Be Your Own Confidence Coach

Be Your Own Confidence Coach

Banish self-doubt and boost self-esteem

Kirsty Ginman

NEW
HOLLAND

This edition first published in 2007 by New Holland Publishers (UK) Ltd
London · Cape Town · Sydney · Auckland
www.newhollandpublishers.com

Garfield House, 86–88 Edgware Road, London w2 2ea, United Kingdom

80 McKenzie Street, Cape Town 8001, South Africa

Unit 1, 66 Gibbes Street, Chatswood, NSW 2067, Australia

218 Lake Road, Northcote, Auckland, New Zealand

isbn 978 1 84537 900 1

Publishing Manager: Jo Hemmings
Project Editor: Camilla MacWhannell
Cover design: Ian Escott
Design: Nicky Barneby
Editor: Deborah Taylor
Production: Joan Woodroffe

Reproduction by Modern Age Repro Co., Hong Kong
Printed and bound in India by Replika Press Pvt. Ltd

For Brian O'Hara with love

Contents

Introduction

World leaders experience moments of low confidence, especially before they are about to address their nation; members of royal families throughout the world have moments of self-doubt when preparing to make public appearances; film stars suffer from anxiety just before they are about to go on set or collect an award and even your boss feels low in confidence at times too. So, you see, you are in very good company and are certainly not alone!

The purpose of this book is to make YOU a much more confident, happy and 'alive' person. I want you to be able to live your life to its fullest and enjoy each day for what it is. By the end of this book, I want you to feel so motivated about life that you could burst, and feel so confident that you can take on anything that life may throw at you.

Firstly though, I want you to understand what confidence is all about and make you realize how you can be completely in control of yours at all times in your life. There are events and experiences from your past that can affect your present level of confidence and there are situations you may find yourself in now that also may be affecting how confident you are. I will explore the whole world of confidence with you and in the process you will discover aspects of your own confidence levels and the many easy, practical ways with which you can improve it.

Build your own

The book is arranged so that each chapter takes you stage by stage through the process of building your own confidence. Firstly, we look at what confidence is and by the end of this chapter you will be able to clarify what your level of confidence is at present, if you don't know already. Then you will explore each exciting stage of confidence building, looking at what may be affecting your confidence at present, and ways that you can build your confidence to new levels and maintain high self-esteem along the way.

This book is not heavy in the theory or psychology of confidence, and you may hear me say that later on in the book, but it's an important point for me to emphasize. I am not a psychologist; I am a confidence coach. Therefore, while I do look into people's pasts to unravel what may be holding them back from being the confident person they want to be today, I also look at individuals for who they are right now and quickly equip them with easy, practical and highly effective techniques to help boost their own confidence levels.

I really believe that people carry too many worries, burdens or regrets with them in the fast-paced, highly pressured world we live in today. This, in turn, can affect an individual's self-esteem, confidence and ultimately their personality and how they live their life. All these worries are stored in our minds, which can determine the way we think. No wonder people walk around looking gloomy, no wonder we are more negative than positive if we carry around all these concerns. Well, I want to put an end to all of that. I want you to feel freer and happier, and I want to give you a new lease of life. I will give you an overhaul of your mind and make sure you finish this book feeling on top of the world!

The power of an open mind

The people who benefit most from my coaching are those who approach the subject of confidence-building with an open mind, who are prepared to put time and effort into practising the techniques I share with them and who are determined to change their lives for the better. They are also prepared to take conscious risks and face their fears to improve their confidence. Now, when I say risks, I can hear some of you thinking, 'Oh no, what is she going to get me to do?' Don't worry. I am not going to ask you to run into your local restaurant naked and get you to order your favourite pizza – of course, if you have the urge to do this, don't let me stop you; we only live once! – but I do want you to try new ways of boosting your confidence, and to step out of your comfort zone and into new territory in order to move forward and reap the rewards. In every case I can recall my clients' fears actually turned out to be much less than they had originally thought they would be, if not non-existent. Their personal 'confidence monsters' did not really exist!

The process of building your confidence starts and ends with YOU. High confidence is inside you right now and is in your hands for the rest of your life; it's up to you whether you choose to tap into it and use it or not.

This book is packed with easy, achievable and highly effective tips and techniques on how to banish self-doubt and boost your confidence and self-esteem. It is essential reading for anyone who is ready to take control of their life, both professionally and personally. Make today the first day of the rest of your new confident and fulfilled life.

1

Change Your Life Today

> *'Self-confidence is the first requisite to great undertakings.'* — Samuel Johnson, 18th-century writer

So you want to be your own confidence coach? Great, I am privileged that you are putting your trust in me to help you achieve this aim. We have all got confidence within us and I firmly believe that we all start off in life with the same potential for confidence and self-esteem. How many babies and toddlers have you met who appear to be thinking negatively about themselves? You never meet a three-year-old who tells you they don't feel very confident, do you? That's because babies and toddlers just get stuck into what they want to do. Unfortunately, we all know how quickly that can change. By the time most children are ready for school, the difference between each child's level of confidence and self-esteem is already apparent.

A *full and happy life*

It would appear that the seeds of our confidence and sense of self worth begin to grow and develop as soon as we start to experience ourselves as individuals. Typically, our confidence then embarks on a roller coaster ride, being cultivated and strengthened one day and knocked back or diminished the next. I do believe, though, that the kind of childhood we experience is particularly important, because it is then that our basic personality traits and habits are formed.

Confidence is an essential ingredient if you are to achieve your true potential – and achieving your true potential will give you confidence. So you see, it's an ongoing cycle. The responsibility for reaching your true potential as an adult falls completely on your shoulders; you cannot blame your childhood for your adult failures. You can build your confidence stage by stage, realizing your capabilities, overcoming hurdles you find along the way and accepting the challenges you face as you go through life. Ask yourself the following question:

'What is stopping me changing my life today?'

Take a moment to block out everything that's going on around you while you read this, because from this moment on, you will be making the decision to change your life and increase your confidence.

If you find that you are coming up with reasons why you can't change your life today in some way, then ask yourself: 'Are they valid reasons or are they excuses?' The two can get confused. I'm a great one for really believing that I have valid reasons for doing or not doing things, when in reality they are just excuses! I cannot think of one reason why you can't change your life from today. Whatever your circumstances, you can make a change to your life instantly – if you want to. All you need to do is make the decision to take control of yourself and you are halfway there. So are you ready? Do you want to change the way you feel and act and gain greater confidence? Yes? Fantastic! Well done.

Reasons and excuses

Have you ever had that nagging feeling that there is something missing in your life, that you are not completely satisfied with your inner self? Maybe you feel that your career or personal life could be more fulfilling, but you are not too sure what to do about it. Many people, from all walks of life, find their life isn't satisfying enough, and that they want something more than they already have, or at least want life to be different.

But for many of us, these thoughts are just that: thoughts. So we simply go through life wishing day after day that things could be different. The trouble is if you go on wishing and not doing anything about it, you will soon feel it is too late to change and then just sit around and wonder: 'What if I had done something about it?' It can be easier to do nothing than to actually take action to make your wishes a reality. I have debated this point with colleagues and friends many times. Some say that if someone really wants to do something they will, and if they don't do anything, then they can't want it badly enough. Others say that if people don't have the confidence to do something, then all the will-power in the world won't make any difference; they will still be unable to achieve their wishes. What do you think?

It is very easy to make up reasons why you are not doing something you should. You may often hear yourself saying things like: 'I'm too old' or 'I don't have enough money' or 'I don't have enough time.' Well, some of this is nonsense and some of it is fact, but you can work to change the facts in most cases. Most reasons you come up with are really just excuses though – it really is up to you and you alone. You can spend your life making excuses about why you can't make changes in your life, or you can use this energy to take steps towards improving things and achieving your goals. The choice really is yours.

I'd like you to think for a moment. If you were writing your own eulogy, what would you want to be written about you, what would you want people to say about you and how you lived your life? Have you ever wondered what people may say about you when you have passed on? It may seem a bit morbid to think about that right now, but it will give you a good idea about where you are in your life at present and where you want to go. Maybe your eulogy would say something like this:

Here lies John Smith who kept making excuses and putting things off until tomorrow.

Or maybe it would say:

Here lies John Smith who lived life to the full and really lived for every moment.

Think about what your eulogy would say if it were written at this moment in time, and think about what you would like it to say instead. Believe me, once you've read this book, practised the techniques and done the exercises, your eulogy will be very different.

Dreams and aspirations

We all have dreams and ambitions and these run through our minds on a regular basis. How many times a day do you catch yourself thinking about all the things you would like to have or to do? Maybe it's when you're experiencing a quiet or boring moment at work, or when you're in the bath or maybe it's last thing at night before you go to sleep. We all dream, and these dreams keep us striving for more out of life and help keep us motivated each day. If you had to list all the things you daydream about, how long would it take you? Have you ever had a go at it? Well, here is your chance, as you're going to try it now.

Why not write down all you want to achieve in life. For many, the events of 11 September 2001 were life-changing. Incidences like those really can stop us in our tracks and make us reflect on where our lives are and where they are going. It can bring the really important things to the forefront of our minds.

Make a list of all the things that you really want to do before it's too late.

- Don't think about it too deeply, just let your mind wander and write whatever comes into your head. You can probably come up with over 50 goals without even trying.

- When you have compiled your list, hold on to it and see how many things you can tick off this year, or in fact this week or this month.

- Why not get a few friends round and make a social occasion out of it? Get everyone round the table to write their list. You'll certainly learn a lot not just about yourself but also about the people around you. How many of you know your family's dreams or your friends' goals in life? You may think you know some of them, but this way you'll find out many more.

- Maybe if you learned more about what your friends' and family's life aims are then you could help them achieve some of their goals, too. How great would that make them feel – and you for that matter?

EXERCISE

Write down your mission statement about your life. Do it in about 40 words or less and see what you come up with. Ask yourself the following questions:

- What are my passions?
- How do I want to live my life?
- What motivates me about life?

I know writing things down seems like a lot of effort. You're probably thinking: 'Oh no, I really can't be bothered' or 'I'll think about it rather than writing it down, it's just the same.' But it isn't and if you can't be bothered to write a list, can you honestly say you can trust yourself to make the effort to do the other exercises that will bring you higher confidence and self-esteem? Sometimes it can help if you write issues down, as they become more real, which means you can deal with them head on. And you may start to realize how irrelevant they are and this will make them even easier to deal with.

Here is my personal mission statement to help you to get started.

> 'I want my life and that of my family to be filled with love, happiness, fun and laughter. I want us to experience new countries, new people and cultures, fun activities and achieve our own individual dreams and goals.'

How was that? Did it take you a while to create it? Don't worry, sometimes it can take a bit of soul-searching to come up with a paragraph that sums up your life and how you want it to be, both now and in the future. Your mission statement can be updated whenever you like, and your goals will probably alter over time. I find writing a mission statement a very useful way of focusing my mind on the present and on my future. It helps me assess whether what I am doing today is contributing to the achievement of my life goals.

Keep a diary

Can you remember what you did last weekend? Can you remember what you did for your last birthday? Can you remember what you did yesterday? If you find it hard to remember what you have been doing over the past few weeks, months or even years then this is perhaps because your life is too hectic or you are not in fact living each moment as fully as you could be. It does take a bit if discipline, but keeping a diary of your day-to-day life is a great way of documenting your activities. It will enable you to look back and see the direction your life is going in. Keep a diary for a while and see how beneficial it is in helping you evaluate and review your life as it happens.

I remember coaching a very busy business professional, and recommending that he keep a diary. He laughed at me at first and said that he didn't have time and he would have to get his assistant to do it for him. I worked on him, though, and eventually he gave in and committed to starting a diary and keeping it going for a month to see whether he found it useful. He contacted me after a month and thanked me for getting him to do this. He said he didn't realize how much time he was spending at work and how little he was seeing his children – he hadn't noticed how much effort was going into his job for too little reward. He realized his life was out of balance and immediately made changes so he could spend more time with his family. It took something this small to make him realize that a major part of his life was suffering, and this was affecting his self-esteem, confidence and overall happiness.

EXERCISE

Keep a diary of your activities, thoughts and feelings for a month. Write down what you do, how you feel about your life and the thoughts that stick in your mind at the end of each day. Commit to doing this for a whole month. You can use a basic note pad to do this exercise, or write it on your computer or in a special diary. Think of it as writing a book about your life for a month. It makes fascinating reading and you can tell a lot about your life when it's finished, such as:

- The direction your life is taking.
- How fulfilled you are at present.
- How your time is spent throughout each day.
- Whether you have a healthy balance between work and private life.
- How often you do something that helps you relax.
- How often you do something that makes you laugh.

- What your feelings are at present.
- What dominates your thoughts each day.

Writing your daily diary can take only minutes, and you can fit it in before you go to sleep.

Have you got the right attitude to build your confidence?

Harvard and Stanford University in the USA reported recently that 85 per cent of the reason a person gets a job and gets ahead in it is due to attitude; and only 15 per cent is as a result of the relevant skills. Interesting, isn't it? In general, we tend to place a lot more importance and spend a lot more money on our education, when our time and energy may be better spent on creating a better attitude. But how many people actually spend money building a positive attitude in themselves?

With the right attitude, you can go a long way in life, like learn new skills so you become good at a job or a life skill. So ask yourself: 'Where do I spend time and effort – on building my knowledge and skills or on building my attitude?' Many people do not spend any time or effort on either but, perhaps, if many more people realized the benefit of developing and maintaining a positive attitude, they would spend more time doing it.

How many times have you been to a restaurant where the food was really tasty, but the attitude of the staff was poor? However good the food is, you probably wouldn't go back to that restaurant would you, because you didn't have a very good experience? Even though the chef cooked you his best dish, it was ruined by the poor attitude of the staff. What about in a clothes store? Again, there are rows of clothes you like the look of and want to try on, but the assistant's negative attitude makes you feel so uncomfortable that you leave without trying anything on. Attitude makes up a large part of confidence building, and we'll cover this in greater depth later on in the book.

Fear of failure

When coaching people, I find that they spend a disproportionate amount of time dwelling on things that they are not good at, blaming themselves or others and regretting actions they have taken in the past. If you measured how much time and effort has been taken up by worry, regret and negative thought so far in your life, it would be frightening. Apparently, we have around 50,000 thoughts running through our minds every day. I estimate that, on average, 80 per cent of these are negative, so just imagine how much negative energy is flowing through your mind. No wonder it can be hard to feel confident when your mind is not tuned into the right channel for confidence to flow.

Failure or fear of failure plays a huge part in our confidence levels. Many of us do not understand that failure is an event, not a person or a permanent personality trait.

> *'Yesterday ended last night and today is a brand new day, and it's yours to do with it as you wish.'*

Preparing for change

We were all born to be winners and I believe you can plan and prepare to win, and then expect to win. Understanding such ideas can help build your confidence enormously.

When approaching such subjects as building your own confidence, or when you are about to start analysing yourself and your characteristics, it is sometimes difficult to get started. This is because change often sets off inbuilt resistance. Don't worry about this, it is perfectly normal and can be overcome easily. It's just your internal mechanism for challenging yourself to see how serious you are about making a personal change. If it happens to show itself in any way, such as feelings of self-doubt, then mentally just push it to one side. Eventually it will go away as you get more focused.

As we get older, we start to think we know it all, or at least know enough to get through life. We tend to have a lax attitude to learning new things. But, why not change your outlook today and view life as one big learning event? Many of us think that once we have left school the only education we have is in life. Well, that is true to an extent, but we also need mental stimulation.

Why not read something inspirational each day? If you read for 20 minutes at just 240 words per minute, you will be able to read 20 200-page books every year. That is 18 more than the average person reads. What a great way to feed your mind in just 20 minutes a day.

From now on, try to start the day and end the day with warming positive thoughts. Happy inspirational messages can (as the medical profession tells us) cause the brain to flood with endorphins.

Learn a new word every day or a new fact every day, and within five years you'll be able to talk confidently about almost anything. With the internet available to most of us now, access to information is so much easier, and don't forget libraries, which are an unlimited source of up-to-date information. You feel so much better when you learn something new; you feel powerful when you are armed with new information. When your vocabulary improves, your IQ rises and gives you a buzz so you'll want to learn more.

Carpe Diem
The Latin phrase meaning 'Seize the day' or 'live for today'.

'Live for now' or 'live for the moment' are phrases that are used all too often and far too lightly. It is an approach to life that my mother instilled in me from a young age. If you begin to take charge of your life and live for today as a result of reading this book, then that's more than enough for me. I am going to be frank now: none of us has a guarantee that we will be here tomorrow, which is why now is all we have. The present is the only time you have for certain, so make something of this moment. Stop putting off until tomorrow what you can start today and make a promise to yourself that from this moment forward you are going to appreciate each day.

Dealing with risk

Achieving any goal requires us to stretch ourselves personally and so aiming for something will always feel like a risk, which is scary. There is a general rule that achievement and improvement come after risk, so it's something we have to live with.

Most of us start out in life with a fantastically open mind towards risk. As children we want to try new things, so we explore places we shouldn't, scare ourselves with films we shouldn't watch and take physical risks when we learn to walk and ride a bike. And we love it all: the feeling of freedom and sense of achievement – it's irreplaceable. Then, at some point between the ages of 5 and 25 we seem to undergo a shift in attitude regarding risk-taking. It's the time when we become concerned about our safety and security. We get into patterns of observing excitement from afar – mainly on television, or by watching our heroes on film, becoming absorbed in soap characters, and becoming more and more inward in our attitude. We don't want to get our clothes dirty, we don't want to mess up our rooms or climb trees.

As a result, life starts to tick by in a very low-key way without much excitement and with very little experience, and, before you know it, you start to regret not having done anything about it. The buzz you get from life comes from doing new things: meeting new people, experiencing new emotions and gaining new knowledge about yourself and life in general. The search for safety and our own security can really restrict our lives. In fact, the more we do, the more the risk is involved. But, it's a fact that winners do take more risks than losers: but that is why they are seen as winners.

Many of us will, no doubt, have experienced some major loss or trauma in our lives: a bereavement, the break-up of a relationship or maybe having to overcome or live with an illness. These very testing times are extremely difficult to deal with, but they can also be the catalyst for positive change. Anyone who has suffered the loss of a family member or friend, or who has suffered injury or illness will know that the sense of loss or suffering can be unbearable at times, but from that experience they know they have gained strength and a desire to live life to the full.

The truth is that it is only when the worst happens that we realize how short life can be and how valuable it is. It can be very easy to live in the past and reflect on all of the good and bad times, but the sadness can be overwhelming at times, and this can knock our ability to be strong and confident in our everyday lives.

The measure of our state of mind, and therefore the measure of our personal effectiveness, is determined by how far we are able to live in the present, regardless of what happened yesterday and what might happen tomorrow. Now is where you and I are. From this point of view, the key to happiness must be in focusing our minds and strength on the present.

Living in the present

So remember to live now. From here on, commit to this. Maybe you could write down this commitment somewhere, so that you'll be able to see it and be reminded of your decision every time you look at it. One client of mine wrote 'live for today' on postcards and stuck them in prominent places all over her home.

Other clients have created symbols to remind them to live for today, using images as diverse as a sunflower, a picture of the Earth, a family photograph, fresh flowers or a colour (one client loved her 'living in the present' colour so much that she used it to decorate her bedroom). Another client had a small symbol tattooed onto his body to act as a constant reminder! So, if creating your own personal reminder is something you'd like to do, first find something that works for you and then give it a go, as it really will give you a nudge when you are not living for the moment. Make sure you do something you are comfortable with – tattoos are not for everyone, after all.

As children we indulged ourselves totally in the present moment. We managed to stay completely absorbed and involved in what we were doing, whether it was drawing a picture, watching an insect or building a sandcastle. But when we grew up, we learned the art of 'thinking' – the process that can make or break our confidence. We can think and worry about many things at once, some very trivial and others more major problems. The trouble is we allow problems and future worries to crowd our present moment, so much so that we can become miserable, unproductive and unhappy. We also learn to postpone our pleasures and ultimately our happiness. We comfort ourselves by thinking that everything will be better in the future, although we have nothing on which to base that assumption.

Let me share an analogy with you and see if you recognize or relate to it. A school pupil thinks: 'When I finish studying and don't have to do what I'm told, then things will be great!', something I remember thinking myself. He leaves school and suddenly realizes he won't be happy until he has left home, found a place of his own and got a job. He gets a job and has to start at the bottom, earning less than he was hoping. Can you see what's happening? He's thinking: 'I can't be happy quite yet.' As the years go by he's constantly postponing his happiness: until he gets engaged, gets married, buys a home, starts a family, puts the kids in school, gets the kids out of school, retires ... But he drops dead before he allows himself to be happy. All his present moments are spent planning for the wonderful future that never arrives because he is too busy putting off to tomorrow what he could have had today.

R.I.P.
Here lies someone who
was going to be
confident tomorrow.

Can you relate to this? Have you been putting off being truly happy and fulfilled until some point in the future? The thing about being happy is that it has to happen in the present, so we need to decide to be happy now, on the journey, and not just when we arrive at the destination. Similarly, we postpone spending time with the people who mean the most to us. A few years ago, a study was carried out in the United States to determine how much quality time fathers spent with their young children. The study showed that the average middle class father only spent about 37 seconds of quality time with his child each day. A frightening result. No doubt, each father intended to spend more time with his children – when the house was finished, when he had less work on, when he felt less tired ... and so on. I'm sure we all have friends we have been meaning to contact, write to or call, and family members we don't get round to seeing as often as we would like to.

Live life

I do believe that many people never really experience life. Andrew Matthews said in his book *Being Happy*: 'most people die at the age of 25, but are not buried until around their mid-seventies.' He is right: many people do not live life to the full, in fact most of us don't even live it half full. Many, if not all of us, have lost touch with the mystery and magic that surrounds us in our everyday lives. But you can change this, and the first step towards living life to the full is simply feeling better about yourself.

Everybody could do with a little more confidence in one or more areas of their life, whether it's at work, in a relationship or when meeting new people. We can all feel under pressure to live up to ideals imposed upon us by our family, colleagues, the media and ourselves. At times, these goals can be unrealistic, but such pressure can cause anxiety and bruise our confidence badly.

I'm a great believer in the 'just do it' attitude and don't think too much about what's involved. I practise what I preach, which is why

I recommend that you do the same. Avoid thinking about your challenges too much, because that's exactly what they are, challenges, and they can be overcome. I believe that if you think too long and hard about things then you can easily put yourself off doing almost anything. Doubts will soon dominate your thinking and, as a result, you'll never move forward. You've probably found yourself thinking too deeply about something in the past. A familiar negative and fearful pattern of thought is: 'What if I lose my job and can't get another one? Then I won't be able to pay the mortgage and I'll lose my house.'

Get the confidence habit

Any problem you dwell upon too much can begin to look too big to solve, when in fact it originally started only as a thought. I believe learning how to be confident is like learning how to drive – or indeed acquiring any new skill. Perhaps you can remember thinking: 'There is no way I am going to get the hang of this, it's impossible! How on earth can I push that peddle down, change gear and at the same time remember to take my foot off the accelerator?' But before you know it, doing all those things at the same time becomes a habit so you don't even have to think about it any more. It's the same with learning to have more confidence: it will become second nature to you once you have got used to having it. Read the ancient Chinese proverb below.

> *I hear I forget,*
> *I see I remember,*
> *I do I understand.*

So, to really understand what this book is about, you need to do something different. If you do it, you'll understand and it will become a habit to do it. Make a commitment to yourself now that you will do the exercises and take note of the recommendations in this book. It's okay to read about them, but practising them really will mean you'll understand them. Furthermore, research gives the following statistics about human performance:

> We remember 10 per cent of what we hear.
> We remember 25 per cent of what we see.
> We remember 90 per cent of what we do.

So whether you read this book straight through from cover to cover or decide to go through it bit by bit, I urge you to 'just do it' and see what happens to your level of confidence. It is important, therefore, to take the ideas in this book and put them into action. Our world rewards action. Learning is great, but action is what gets results and helps things move forward.

Happy, confident people know that there are no guarantees to the duration of this adventure called life. They also know that this goes for everyone else too. Happy, confident people don't wait until tomorrow to let the people they love know that they love them, they don't postpone watching a beautiful sunset, visiting the countryside or playing with their children. Happy, confident people enjoy whatever they happen to be doing. If they are making sales calls to prospective clients, they vow to enjoy themselves talking to each person, even if what they happen to be doing is called work. If you live each day as if it were your last, when your last day arrives you will have no regrets.

> *'Self-confidence is the result of a successfully survived risk.'*
> — Jack Gibb, 20th-century writer

Having the right attitude to building your confidence is half the challenge. If you sit and read this book with the wrong attitude you won't achieve half as much as you would if you kept an open – and positive – attitude. The right attitude will create a desire within you to really build your confidence to new heights. The fact that you are reading this book means you have decided that you want to increase your confidence. The quick exercise that follows will help you focus your mind on the task ahead.

Write down exactly what it is that you want to achieve. For example, to have greater confidence in all you do. Read the example below as a guide, but please complete your own list as well. I have listed 10 examples, but I know you will come up with many more for yourself. Divide the page in half and write on the left-hand side: 'If I do it, what results will I see?' On the right put: 'If I don't do it, what results will I see?' Then write down all the reasons you can think of for each statement.

GOAL: I WANT TO ACHIEVE GREATER CONFIDENCE IN ALL I DO

If I do it, what results will I see?	If I don't do it, what results will I see?
High self-esteem	Low self-esteem
Greater confidence	Low confidence
Feel happier	Feel unhappy
Career success	Limiting career potential
New experiences	Little or no new experiences
Inner contentment	Inner frustration
More friends	Limited opportunities to meet new friends
More acquaintances	Few acquaintances
Healthier lifestyle	Possible stress related health issues
Personal satisfaction	Personal disappointment

It is plain to see that the benefits of making this change in your life far outweigh the disadvantages. There really is nothing stopping you from building your confidence today: the only person holding you back is you.

Summary

The truth is that we have a choice between really living or merely existing. Driving a car can be a risk, having children can be a risk, eating in a restaurant can be a risk – even though some risks are greater than others, in general, life is a risk. So get out there and live, be as happy and fulfilled as you can using your increased confidence as a guide. Jump into life with both feet, live in the present and while you may be waiting for certain wishes to come true, do something else that makes you feel good. In fact, pause for a moment and think about all the things that make you feel happy, excited and content. I hope there is a big grin on your face right now as those happy, possibly cheeky, thoughts run through your mind!

By now, I hope you are feeling motivated and ready to start making a difference in your life. You really won't regret building your confidence because having it will open up many more opportunities for you, so let's get on with it right now.

2

What Is Confidence?

'The man who has confidence in himself gains the confidence of others.' — Hasidic saying

If you asked most people whether they wanted to increase their confidence level they would all probably say, 'Yes'. It seems that whatever you want to achieve in this world, having confidence gives you a head start and allows you to experience much more of life. If you want to be successful at work or comfortable and relaxed in relationships or at home in social gatherings, then it is essential you have confidence in yourself and your ability to go about doing things.

The definition of confidence

Before we go any further let's define confidence. The dictionary definition is 'a feeling of reliance or self certainty, a sense of self-reliance'. The word derives from the Latin *confido* – to put one's trust or faith in someone.

Confidence therefore means 'to put trust in yourself'. It is not synonymous with arrogance, bragging, overbearing, boasting, pretentiousness or superiority. People with confidence feel secure about themselves; they come across as relaxed and comfortable and have a willingness to learn from others. They also appear interested in what others have to say and interact well with people they meet. Let's take a look at some more examples of the characteristics of confidence:

- Believing in your own ability.
- Having the courage to achieve what you want.
- Believing that you are as capable as the next person.
- Being secure and relaxed about yourself.
- Having the ability to act confidently when you're feeling low.
- Acknowledging when you have made a mistake.
- Not worrying about what other people think of you.
- Not letting anyone intimidate you.
- Having the ability to talk to anyone about anything.
- Feeling happy and contented within yourself.
- Having the ability to live for the moment.
- Having the ability to focus on the future.

You have a whole range of tools, strengths, skills, abilities and strategies available to you, which will enable you to enhance your confidence, but sometimes you may not be fully aware of them. The great thing is that they are all inside you just waiting to get out – so it's down to you to invite them out to play. By becoming more aware of these tools and the way you can apply them, you can start to build your confidence. Have a go at the confidence checker below and see how you do. This is just a very basic way of assessing your levels of confidence at the moment.

EXERCISE

Complete the following short quiz to discover your current confidence levels.

1. Do you really enjoy life?
   A. No, nowhere near as much as I should.
   B. Sometimes, it depends how I feel.
   C. Most of the time, I love life.

2. Do you enjoy meeting new people?
   A. No, not at all, I dread it.
   B. Occasionally, but I get very nervous.
   C. Yes, I usually look forward to it.

3. Can you walk into a room full of strangers and feel instantly comfortable?
   A. No, I want the ground to open up and swallow me.
   B. I can, but generally walk round the edges and look at the floor.
   C. Yes, I normally mix really well.

4. Do you find it easy to make conversation with a broad selection of people?
   A. No, I try to avoid it like the plague.
   B. I can only make conversation with people I know at my own level.
   C. Yes, I enjoy mixing with all types of people.

5. Do you feel you are always relaxed in social situations?
   A. No, I'm never relaxed in social situations.

B. If I know people, I'm okay.

C. I love social situations, as I get to meet new people.

6. Do you think positively about yourself most, if not all, of the time?
   A. No, hardly ever.
   B. Sometimes, if I'm in the right frame of mind.
   C. Yes, as this helps me stay positive and confident.

7. When thinking about your future, do you feel excited about what's to come?
   A. No, I can't think about anything exciting that might happen.
   B. I sometimes wonder what good things are around the corner.
   C. I believe the best is yet to come in my life.

8. If you went for a job interview, but did not get it, would you...
   A. Blame yourself, be down about it and give up trying to get that type of job.
   B. Put it down to experience, think about trying again in the future.
   C. Ask the interviewer for feedback, learn from the experience and try again.

9. How do you rate your knowledge and outlook on personal development?
   A. I learned all I need to know to get through life at school.
   B. I would like to learn something new but don't know how to go about it.
   C. I am keen to learn as much about life, people and the world as I can.

10. What sort of people do you admire?
    A. People who generally tick along in life.
    B. People who try occasionally to better themselves.
    C. People who strive for their goals, even if they don't always achieve them.

HOW DID YOU SCORE?

A – If you find that you generally choose A, then I suggest your confidence is very low, and you are not living and enjoying life as fully as you have a right to. Your negative attitude to life is driving your confidence to very low levels, depriving you of the self-esteem you want to experience.

B – If you find that you mainly choose B, then you do have confidence and self-esteem, but it is not as high as it could be. I suggest that you take some time out to work on your own confidence so you can enjoy life more. You do have a positive attitude occasionally but this needs fine-tuning so you can really experience life to the full.

C – If you mainly choose C, then you certainly have the right attitude to life and certainly have the desire to think positively. All you may need now are some techniques to help you feel confident in whatever situation you find yourself.

Confidence and self-esteem

Having confidence is vital for success and true happiness. Anything is possible when you're feeling good about yourself, just as everything will seem beyond your reach when your confidence is low. Poor confidence comes hand in hand with low self-esteem, and it is at the root of many of our problems. It can ruin relationships and careers, cause self-destructive patterns and hold us back from achieving our potential. The beginnings of poor self-esteem and low confidence usually stem from childhood, but it can be damaged again in our adult life. Unfortunately, even if we had an emotionally balanced childhood our confidence still has to survive the assault of modern adult life.

Confident people understand either instinctively or because they have developed an inner belief, that it is much more beneficial to enjoy life than to think about it too deeply. If you are constantly analysing your life, you will always be able to find fault with what you are doing, causing yourself unnecessary worry and undue stress.

When you are feeling low in confidence, it can be hard to find the motivation you need to complete tasks, so you may feel hesitant about attempting some of the exercises and techniques presented here. Don't worry or feel overwhelmed by any of them, take them at your own pace and give each exercise the 100 per cent that it and you deserve.

> *'Confidence like art never comes from having all the answers, it comes from being open to all the questions.'*
> — Earl Gray Stevens, writer

If you build your confidence, it will bring you better self-esteem, mental and physical health and well-being. It will help you in creating new and improved friendships and relationships both professionally and personally. Increased confidence and self-esteem will help you live a happy family life full of new and exciting experiences. It will bring with it a successful working life where you will achieve your potential. In fact, increased confidence will help you take your life down the path you want it to go.

What causes loss of confidence?

If you feel that at the moment more is required of you than you are able to give when faced with a challenge, you are likely to feel less in control, more anxious, more helpless and more stressed.

Being fired or made redundant, failing an exam or being rejected by someone tends to dent our confidence. In all these situations we're at the mercy of someone else – we feel powerless and at times probably quite worthless. That sounds depressing, but the great thing is there's a lot that we can do to put that right straight away. The good news is, if you focus on your strengths, your skills and your general ability to cope with the situation – even if you can't change it – your feelings towards the challenge of moving forward is likely to be much more positive.

This holds true even when you're facing a situation you haven't encountered before, or when you're in a familiar situation that you didn't handle particularly well in the past.

It's not unusual to feel confident in some areas of your life but less confident in others. This may be in your personal relationships (partners, friends and family), or at work (when talking with your boss or adapting to a new job). Low confidence levels can also affect your behaviour with your family or times when you encounter new people.

For example, a successful business person may find it difficult to relate intimately to a partner in a close relationship or a member of their family but may be charming when they're at work. A skilled footballer may find it difficult to become a football coach after he has retired from being a player. An actor may find it easy to perform on stage but get tongue tied when chatting to someone in a bar or meeting people for the first time. An adult who is perfectly confident with their friends may find it hard to stop their parents treating them like a child. All these scenarios are very common and perfectly normal.

Everyone has moments in their lives when they feel they lack confidence. This is because things that cause us to be low in confidence, are generally much the same from one person to another, whatever the situation. It's true that some people lack confidence due to past traumatic experience, and these people may need more help or different tactics to regain their confidence. But there are some key reasons why people lack confidence and once you know about these, you can start building your confidence immediately.

Research has proven that our mental well-being affects our physical well-being. Psychological research shows that lack of confidence can be a habit, like eating too much or biting your nails. To overcome any habit, first you must change the way you think about it, so from now on you must change the way you think about your lack of confidence, turn your negative thoughts into positive ones and take action to make changes. Just watch your confidence soar as you try new things. At the end of this book, YOU will be the expert in confidence building, and will be able to control your own life like never before.

If you don't have any confidence in yourself, you can become invisible. Opportunities may pass you by, your potential is wasted and you avoid new experiences because you don't put yourself forward. You feel as if you have no control over your life. But you do, it's just that you are not in tune with the power you really have over yourself.

We all need more confidence so we can speak out for ourselves and not be put upon by others. Do you ever find that you walk away from a situation and say to yourself: 'I wish I had said that, I can't believe I didn't speak up for myself'? Maybe you feel you are not confident enough to complain about a bad meal or service in a restaurant or you are not confident enough to return faulty goods to a shop. Well that will change when you are a confident, happy person.

We come into contact with many different types of people on a daily basis and our confidence levels vary accordingly. Some people intimidate us and others encourage us. Usually, though, everyone else seems confident when we don't. But the people we admire for their confidence may not be as confident as we think they are. Something I often hear people say is: 'Even though everyone at work thinks I'm a very confident person, I'm not really.' Often, even though someone seems confident, underneath they feel insecure.

Shy and fearful people hide behind a veneer of confidence and find it difficult to admit to themselves how they are feeling. However, lack of confidence can reveal itself in many ways – arrogance, bullying, aggressiveness, over-optimism and an overbearing attitude.

When we are younger we are greatly influenced by what goes on around us and we learn to be insecure in response to events we experience. Let's take a look at what knocks our confidence and self-esteem when we are younger. Below are just a few examples:

- Being put down, ridiculed or humiliated.
- Being told things like: 'You've never been very good with numbers.'
- Being told that we are like someone: 'You're headstrong and stubborn, just like your father.'

- Having your feelings persistently ignored or denied, such as a parent not noticing how you feel.
- Being told how to feel: 'You shouldn't be sad about that, it's only _____ you ought to be excited.'
- Not having your basic needs met. When, for example, younger brothers and sisters receive more love and attention, or different races and classes receive privileges above your own.

Unfortunately, even if you led a charmed life your confidence and self-esteem still have to be tough to survive modern life. Everyday occurrences can knock your confidence without realizing it. The following are examples of how your confidence may have been dented in the last day, or month. Do you recognize any of them?

- Being taken for granted.
- Being put down.
- Putting on weight and/or getting spots.
- Being deceived by someone.
- Being criticized by someone.
- Failing tests or interviews.
- Other people being promoted around you.
- Being turned down for a job.
- Not getting the pay rise or appreciation for your work.
- Losing a job.
- Relationship breakdown.

These are just a few of the more common examples, but of course there are many others. Have any of the above happened to you recently? Don't be surprised if they have – most, if not all, of us experience at least some of these things at some time or other in our life. Some may happen more frequently than others, but all are major contributing factors in reducing our confidence.

What knocks your confidence? We need to become much more aware of the things that bring us down and affect our self-esteem so that we can deal with them as soon as they happen. Take a moment to think about some of the factors that can knock your confidence then write them down so you can identify them clearly as you work through the book.

> *'Life is a series of experiences, each one makes us bigger, even though sometimes it's hard to realize this.'*
> — Henry Ford, Industrialist

What does confidence look like?

People in this world come in all shapes, sizes, characters and personalities. Let's take a moment to have a look at some of the more common characteristics of people with different levels of confidence.

Mr, Mrs or Miss 'Highly Unconfident'

They display some if not all of the following behaviours:

- Quiet, hardly speaks a word to anyone.
- Little or no eye contact with people around them.
- Stand back from the crowd and hide behind people or objects.
- Blush and look at the floor for most of the time when in company.
- Shy body-language, have nervous habits such as nail biting or twiddling thumbs.
- May not have too many friends, as socializing is difficult for them.

Can you relate to any of the characteristics of the above profile?

Mr, Mrs or Miss 'Slightly Confident'

They display some if not all of the following behaviours:

- Speak when spoken to but not often volunteering conversation.
- Have some eye contact and smile occasionally when speaking to you.
- Mix with people at gatherings but are not the life and soul of the party.
- Will appear quite relaxed and happy with their own company.
- Polite and enjoy listening to others speak.
- Will have quite a few close friends.
- Their body language is quite relaxed but not too open and confident.

Can you relate to any of the characteristics of the above profile?

Mr, Mrs or Miss 'Highly Confident'

They display some if not all of the following behaviours:

- Always chatting to people, the main instigator in conversations.
- Direct eye contact, nodding when people speak and smiling a lot.
- Tactile, may touch other people when interacting with them.
- Very sociable and enjoy meeting new people.
- Mix easily within circles of people.
- Have many friends and acquaintances.
- Ask people questions and are interested in them.
- Very relaxed and confident body language.

Can you relate to any of the above characteristics of the above profile? If not, don't worry because by the end of this book these behaviours will be available for you to draw upon should you want to.

In the profiles on pages 39 and 40, I have highlighted the common behaviours in people with varying confidence levels. The problem, though, is that confidence can be displayed in many different ways, just like a lack of it. You may know someone who displays many of the confident characteristics and so you assume they are highly confident, yet if you asked them how confident they really feel, their answer may surprise you.

I have worked with some very successful people, from well-known, high-profile celebrities, to high-powered chief executives of international companies. You would probably assume that all these people would ooze confidence and you may wonder why they needed to see a confidence coach. But some people hide behind a veneer of confidence when inside they don't feel confident at all, and they lack self-esteem. As a result, they have to 'act' confident in their jobs. While 'acting' confident is fine and can get the job done, it is tiring and not very comfortable.

The aim of becoming fully versed in the techniques laid out in this book is that you will allow your confidence levels to increase and become part of your natural way of being. The great thing about this is that you will not have to try to be confident, you will feel it inside you and it will be natural and easy.

Being really confident is all about liking yourself, feeling comfortable with yourself and being confident in your abilities to deal with any situation that may arise. Many people have told me how much they dislike themselves, particularly when they are lacking confidence. Their self-esteem is rock bottom and they just want to be someone else. That 'someone else' can be somebody they know, somebody famous or just anyone. One client once told me: 'I don't care who I am, as long as I'm not me.' People who feel this way are often very hard on themselves and constantly critical. They blame themselves for mistakes they have made and decisions they have taken. In general, they carry around a sense of deep self-loathing.

When we are unhappy, we can be really cruel to ourselves, which is very destructive to our self-esteem and confidence. This is something that we all need to be aware of as we can be far too hard on ourselves when we don't need to be.

EXERCISE

Create a character in your mind who is your own best friend. Now imagine you have stepped out of your own body and that you are standing next to or opposite yourself in the body of that character. Take a look at yourself for a moment and think about what type of person you see; think of all the good things about this person in front of you. Think about some of the kind things this person has done for others. What was the last gift this person bought someone? What words of comfort and encouragement can you give to this person standing in front of you. Treat them as if they are your best friend. When they ask for advice and support, what do you say to them? Do you hold their hand, put your arm around them or hug them? Talk to them in the same caring way that you would to your best friend.

This is a very simple way to make yourself feel better about who you are. From now on, do it whenever you start giving yourself a hard time about something. Recognize the habit and stop. This will raise your self-esteem and will build your confidence.

EXERCISE

When you next get a moment to yourself have a look at yourself in a mirror. Take a moment to think about the sort of person you see. Look beyond what you initially see and take a deeper look at yourself 'behind the mask'. This may feel uncomfortable at first, especially if it's a day when you are feeling low in confidence and self-esteem. Remember that we can all be very hard on ourselves and very self-critical and that we usually find it easier to think about all the things that are wrong with us than all the things that are good about us. However, when we look at the negative feelings we have about ourselves, we often find that they are superficial and that they have no foundation in reality. Some negative feelings may linger on from the past, especially if we have been criticized by someone who is important to us, like a teacher, your parents or your partner.

What we believe affects everything we do in the present, and stays with us until we do something about it. So you need to change your negative beliefs about yourself in order to build your confidence to new heights. Most, if not all, negative beliefs we have about ourselves are not true, because generally we are not rude, unkind, stupid, worthless or any of the other negativities we may throw at ourselves.

Character types

Earlier on, we looked at the characteristics of people with different levels of confidence. In truth, it is almost impossible to pigeonhole every single person because everyone is unique and has a distinct personality. Your personality hugely influences your confidence and the way you come across to others. We are all a mixture of different characteristics so you need to be realistic about who you are and how you can get the result you want.

Trying to become the most confident person in the world overnight will put you under too much pressure. First, get to know the type of person you are now so that you can begin to change into the type of person you want to be. Let's take a look at more profile types; maybe you will recognize parts of yourself in some or all of them.

The shy, retiring type

Shy, retiring characters know what they want out of life, but usually don't have the confidence or motivation to achieve it. They don't like to get in other people's way, and prefer to be quiet when in company. They think of others much more than they do themselves and so they put the feelings of others before their own. They don't face things head on but avoid confrontation and any situation that may make them feel uncomfortable. They don't take control of their own life, they allow external forces to dictate to them how things are going to be. These people feel that when they are assertive, it actually comes across as aggressive, which is the worst feeling in the world for them. Often, one or both of their parents is a dominating character and maybe very aggressive and so shy, retiring people do their best to behave in the opposite way to their parents.

The victim or self-pitying type

Victims or self-pitying types have the lowest self-esteem of all the characters. They are constantly focused on the negative and they often cannot see anything remotely positive about their life. They have spent most of their life dealing with the needs of others to the point where they have lost their own identity and forgotten their own goals. These people are constantly in the background and don't believe they have anything interesting to say. They are constantly putting themselves down and cannot deal with compliments in any way at all. Their favourite words are 'can't' and 'should', and they are pessimistic by nature.

The bully or aggressive type

Bullies or aggressive types are often very insecure about themselves and use confrontation to hide their insecurity. Deep down, they are often very angry people who harbour a lot of regrets and bad feeling about their past or the way they have been treated. They believe that aggression will get them what they want from life, and have no consideration for other people's feelings. They often brag about what they have achieved or what they are doing. They also like the sound of their own voice and are very bad listeners as they have no interest in other people at all. They generally like being in control and don't mind stepping on other people to get what they want.

The depressed or very low self-esteem type

The depressed or very low self-esteem types have lost their zest, excitement and enthusiasm for life. For much, if not all, of the time their energy levels are very low. They have extremely low self-esteem and almost no confidence. They hide behind inactivity hoping this will keep them away from people and out of the spotlight.

The excitable and enthusiastic type

The excitable and enthusiastic type seems only to see the positives in anything they do or other people do. They gush with enthusiasm at everything and get excited at the smallest of events or activities. They are fully tuned-in to the joys of life and try desperately to get others to share their joy. They have a 'let's just do it' attitude and find negative and depressed people frustrating. They are full of energy and great fun to be with but they can be tiring if you are with them for too long. They are hugely optimistic and can only see the good in life and other people.

The emotional, abusive type

The emotional, abusive type likes to control others, both mentally and physically, if they can. They have a knack of draining the self-esteem out of others and often leave them feeling low in confidence. They are very good with words and try to outwit anyone they meet. They are self-obsessed and don't have the ability to care for others' feelings. They live off the energy and emotions of others, leaving them feeling zapped of energy. They never think they are in the wrong and play mental games with people, so it is always someone else's fault. They thrive in and perpetuate the blame culture.

The confident and high self-esteem type

The confident and high self-esteem type has learned to like themself, and sometimes, even better, love themself. This type of person is fine-tuned to their own feelings and those of others. They like to speak openly and share knowledge as well as listen carefully and intently to others. They don't need to show off as they are secure in their own abilities. They are very balanced characters and treat others with respect. They are fully aware of their own characteristics and are able to put them into perspective. These people don't let other people knock their confidence as they have an inner contentment and are happy with who they are.

We are all very different characters and our personalities evolve over time. When you look back over your life and remember how you used to behave when you were younger, do you sometimes cringe when you recall the way you used to act in certain situations? Rather than cringing, though, use this perspective to remind yourself that if you have changed from that old behaviour to a new behaviour, you can do it again now. After all, it's never too late to learn, grow and change for the better, if you want to.

If you identified with one or more of the character types above, you may now want to consider whether you are happy being that way or whether you are ready to make a change.

EXERCISE

If possible, ask a close friend or family member to help you with this. If not, or you don't feel comfortable talking openly about your confidence levels with someone else, then do this exercise on your own.

Take another look at the profiles above and write down any of the characteristics that you see in yourself. Identify the ones you want to change, the ones that make you feel unhappy and the ones that lower your self-esteem. If your family or friends are helping you with this exercise, discuss each characteristic you have identified separately and look at why you are not happy being like this. Discuss how it makes you feel, and how it affects your private and working lives.

Using the table below as a guide, write down each characteristic and how it impacts on your life.

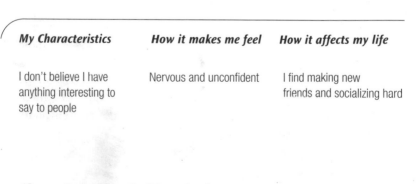

My Characteristics	How it makes me feel	How it affects my life
I don't believe I have anything interesting to say to people	Nervous and unconfident	I find making new friends and socializing hard

| I become nervous when speaking in public | Stressed, sick and anxious | I am not selected to give presentations at work. I am no good in interviews |
| I'm not comfortable giving eye contact to people | Nervous and threatened | People don't speak to me as they must think I'm unapproachable |

Ask your friend or family member for their opinion on your characteristics, as they may see you very differently to the way you see yourself. They may also be able to help you define the way you behave or come across to others. It's very useful to get a second opinion from someone who knows you well because we tend to exaggerate what we think of as our bad points because of our negative feelings about ourselves.

If you are doing this exercise on your own, first identify the characteristics you are not happy with, then make sure they are clear in your mind so you can refer to them throughout the book. Use this exercise to get to know what it is about yourself that you are unhappy with, so you can tackle it as you go through the book.

Summary

As we come to the end of this chapter, remind yourself what the ultimate aim is – to build your confidence and self-esteem in order to feel happy and be more successful at whatever it is you want to achieve.

It's interesting to ask people you know what confidence means to them, as you'll see that there may be many different interpretations. It is therefore important that you know what confidence means to you and what it is that you are unhappy about in yourself at the moment so that you can start to tackle it now.

Confidence is only a word, yet the feelings that go with it can be very powerful. Don't be afraid of it, though. Many people have told me that even the word feels daunting and too much to deal with at times. Think of the word 'confidence' as an exciting experience you have yet to explore, and that greater confidence will enrich your life. Greater confidence is the ticket to a full and rewarding existence. Think about this book as a ticket to higher confidence. Remember that building confidence happens bit by bit and layer by layer.

One of the key ingredients to having greater confidence is to live in the present and look forward to the future rather than looking back at the past. But in order to understand who you are now and why you lack confidence, it is necessary to look into the past and explore whether earlier experiences may have knocked your confidence without you realizing it. But we must only look back occasionally and only in order to gain greater confidence for the present and the future.

3

Leave Your Past Behind

'Experience tells you what to do, confidence allows you to do it.' — Stan Smith, sportsman

When a captive elephant is young, its leg is chained to a large stake to prevent it from escaping. However hard the elephant pulls to free itself, it can't get away. Eventually, the elephant gives up.

Then, a thin piece of rope is put around its foot and attached to a weak cane. What stops the elephant pulling free now is just the belief that pulling won't have any effect on the rope. It has been conditioned to believe that anything tied around its leg, however flimsy, will prevent it from escaping, so it no longer tries.

The point is a simple one: if you let go of your past and challenge your thinking about the world you can overcome anything that holds you back so that you can move forward. There is a saying that states: 'If you always do what you've always done, you'll always get what you've always got.' If you change the way you act or react in a particular situation, you will change your life and your perception of what you can achieve.

Think for a moment about how you behave when your confidence is low. Maybe you always behave in the same way in a particular situation or react a certain way about an event because you have always done it that way. Now is the time to challenge the way you do things as this is just a habit. Like the elephant, you too have been conditioned. Let's look at some examples of how conditioning can affect our behaviour and confidence levels.

Example 1: John and his sister Mary

John was frequently told by his parents that his younger sister Mary was the brighter of the two of them, even though John has a good level of intelligence. Mary frequently teased John about being stupid. As a result, John grew up believing that he was. He failed his exams and left school as early as he could. As an adult, John always puts himself down in conversation, saying things like: 'I've never been very bright', 'I'll be useless in that pub quiz', 'I'd never be able to do a job where I have to use my brain.' John has now realized that he allowed the belief that he is stupid to dictate what he did with his life because his confidence was knocked from a young age.

Example 2: Debbie, a full-time mum

Debbie is a full-time mum and realizes that when her children grow up and leave home in a few years time, she will want to get a job that will allow her some freedom, an income and the opportunity to meet new people. When she discusses this idea with her husband and her friends and family, they all tell her that she would find it difficult to get a job as she has never had one before. Some people even laugh at the thought of her working. Debbie allows this judgement from those around her to deter her from thinking about getting a job. A few years on and Debbie finds herself 'home alone' and has now realized that she let the opinions of those around her knock her confidence and condition her into believing she would be unsuccessful in a career. She thoroughly deserves the opportunity to find work but has allowed the opinions of others to get in her way.

Example 3: Mike can't find a girlfriend

Mike was a tall, thin teenager who had a large, fun-loving crowd of friends. They all went to the same school. For years, all his friends teased Mike about the fact that he was tall and thin, saying he would never find a girlfriend as 'girls like men with muscles'. Mike found himself starting to believe this, so he did not even try to meet a girl, even though all his friends were dating. Mike allowed himself to become 'conditioned' to believe he would not find a girlfriend. To make matters worse, his friends kept reminding him by saying: 'See, we were right all along!' This innocent teasing caused Mike to lose his confidence around women.

Example 4: Neil finds it difficult to show his feelings

Neil grew up in a 'happy' family. However, it was a household where very little affection was shown by his parents. Neil received love and affection from his parents but he rarely saw any show of tactile affection, such as hugging. Neil, now in his adult years and in a relationship himself, has difficulty showing affection to his partner, who experiences a lot of frustration as a result. Neil finds it exceptionally difficult to share affection because he has not been conditioned to do so.

A lot of what has happened to us in the past affects how we act and think today, it is a fact that upbringing plays a major part in our make-up and that this, in turn, determines our confidence levels. In order to move forward in our lives and achieve new things, we need to release the past. If we free up some space in our heads and hearts, we are more likely to be able to embrace the present and the future.

Internal spring cleaning

Getting stuck in the past and in old behaviour patterns is a bit like wearing the same old clothes year after year. At first, it isn't too bad; the fashion changes and you look a bit out of date but nothing more than that. However, as time goes by, the clothes become too small and shabby. Eventually, you just don't feel good wearing them but they're all you've got. Even efforts to change and collect new outfits don't work because you can't seem to discard the old ones. Your wardrobe is cluttered and overfull so it becomes easier to wear the same familiar things over and over again. These outfits now define who you are, so when you look in the mirror you no longer think about changing what you see. When you clear out your wardrobe, you finally assess our old clothes and throw many of them away to make room for some new and different ones; clothes that give you a new identity. You vow to keep yourself up to date in the future.

It's the same with the mind; it needs a good clear out from time to time. To do this, you need to acknowledge that your past has happened and is finished so you can accept that what's done is done. There may be some past experiences that you regret or look back on in a negative way. I do believe that all of us have things in our past that we regret or wish hadn't happened. We may wish that we had acted differently in a relationship, taken different decisions about our career or maybe not treated someone as we did. But, in reality, hanging onto regrets is very unproductive and a waste of energy.

What you can do now is to learn from your past so you can do something different in future. Reviewing how you think and feel in certain situations takes getting used to, but if you do it, you'll find that as you challenge what you think, you'll eventually change what you believe.

Ditching emotional baggage

You are probably familiar with the term 'emotional baggage'. To me, it sums up what the past feels like. We all know that as we go through life we meet different people and experience a variety of emotions. As a result, we end up carrying around or holding onto many thoughts and feelings that weigh us down. Hanging on to old emotions, regrets and sadness holds us back from experiencing new thoughts and feelings.

If there's too much emotional baggage in your head – and your heart – you may find it difficult to concentrate on the here and now. We spend a large proportion of our time cleaning our houses or our cars but we don't spend any time clearing out our minds. It's healthy to have a spring clean of our hearts and minds now and then, in order to free up some space for new thoughts and feelings. After all, we go to the dentist to care for our teeth, the doctor to care for our body, the hairdresser to care for our hair, so why shouldn't we take care of our mind in the same way?

Many of us ignore this aspect of our welfare and continue to take on board more and more negative thoughts and limiting beliefs each day, filling our minds – like we fill our wardrobes – until they are bursting with redundant ideas. Of course, I'm not saying you should forget people and emotions from your past, after all, they make us who we are today, but I do believe we can deal with those old thoughts and feelings for what they are: baggage that holds us back.

EXERCISE

Now is the time to start recognizing those old ideas and negative experiences, thoughts or feelings that are weighing you down. Take a look at some of these examples of emotional baggage and see how pointless they are:

- I wish I was still with my old partner – we were happy together, really.
- I wish I had taken that job – things would be so different now if I had.
- I wish I had bought that house – it would be worth a fortune now!

- I regret having finished that relationship. My life was so much fun then.

- I was really silly to have cheated on my partner. I can't believe I did that!

- If only I'd passed my exams I would be able to get all sorts of great jobs now.

- I really wish I hadn't sold my car – it was my prize possession.

- Why did I pass up that opportunity to go abroad? Things would be so different if I'd gone.

- Why didn't I say what I felt at the time? If I had, maybe my boss would respect me more now.

- Why didn't I listen to my intuition, I wouldn't be in this situation now if I had.

- Why didn't I visit them more? It would have made them so happy.

- I should have helped mum more – she did so much for me.

- Why wasn't I there for my friends when they needed me?

- If only I had said the right thing to him and not been so preoccupied with my own problems.

Now write down your own regrets or emotional baggage. See how many you come up with – you may be surprised at how many you write down once you get going. Have a think about it, and see if anything else springs to mind. Are you still holding onto feelings about someone or something that is no longer relevant in your life? Is it time to admit to yourself that it's over or it's in the past, or just understand that you took the decision at the time for whatever reason and now you have to move on?

If you know a relationship is over then ditch the lingering thoughts from the past and move forward from today. If you believe there is still a chance to rekindle that relationship then do something about it, take some action and stop wondering 'what if'. If you are single but are still thinking about your ex-partner, then you give off the wrong signals to potential new partners. As soon as you leave the past behind, you will give off a very different aura, and you'll meet someone new.

Do you spend too much time thinking about a promotion or new job you didn't get and keep wondering why you were not offered it? Do you punish yourself for flunking an interview? Maybe you answered a question wrong or didn't perform well on the day. Well stop right now, as you are not doing yourself any good. All this negative, reflective thinking will be driving your confidence even lower. Learn from the experience in order to deal with it in a more productive way next time. If you feel you performed well and don't know why you were not offered the position, then if it's not too late, call and ask for feedback. If it was some time ago then I would put it down to just not being right for you at the time. 'What will be will be' as I was always told as a child, really does help me as an adult. If it's just not meant to be, maybe there's something better around the corner. Thinking this way can also ease the pressure you put on yourself to get everything you go for. Sometimes you can try too hard. All this tension puts you in the wrong frame of mind to succeed and does you more harm than good. What's more, you are unlikely to be in the right state of mind to approach the situation positively.

We make many decisions as we go through life. What would happen if we hung on to every regret about every decision that didn't work out as we wanted? It would be impossible to carry around all our regrets, wouldn't it? Hanging onto regrets for too long, talking about the past all the time, bearing grudges and holding on to feelings of betrayal or bitterness is not good for us, especially if we bottle up these negative emotions and never let them out. Decisions you have made in life that you really regret will come to mind occasionally, but, from now on, make a conscious effort to clear them away. Rationalize your thoughts so you don't get caught up in the emotions.

EXERCISE

This exercise is designed to clear away your past regrets once and for all. Use the chart below as a guide and fill in your own regrets and complete each box as shown in the example. Think about each regret and the positives that may have come out of that experience.

My Emotional Baggage	What I regret	A positive part of the experience	What have I learned?
My last personal relationship	Ending it	Having many happy times	To be more true to my feelings
Not getting the job I went for	Not presenting myself better at the interview	Interview experience: will help me with the next one	I need to come across as more confident
I should have been there for my friend in her time of need	Not supporting her through her trauma	Realizing how much she means to me	To always be there for my friends
I didn't visit my parents enough	Not supporting or being there for them as often as I could have	My parents realize how full my life is and how hard I work	To balance what is important to me in both my private and professional lives
I should have left education with more qualifications	Not going to university to take a degree	Starting my working career early and earning money	That I want to take a degree to achieve my dream
I was bullied at school	Not defending myself and allowing others to push me around	Gradually gaining strength to overcome the bullies and realize they were wrong	To not take the bullies' comments personally
I haven't travelled abroad as much as I wanted	Not taking up the opportunity to travel when I was younger	Feeling the potential excitement of visiting new countries	I want to travel more, and need to focus on achieving this

How did you get on? It is a good idea when going through the confidence-building process to get rid of your past gremlins, or the skeletons in your cupboard. Release them so that you free up some space for more exciting and rewarding thoughts and feelings.

Rather than dwelling on the negative aspects of 'What if' or 'I wish I had', look at what it is you regret and then do something about it. If you can't do anything about your regrets, for example, you didn't buy the house that is now worth a fortune or you didn't go out with the person you wanted to and now they are in a relationship with someone else, then learn from it, accept you did what you did at the time for a reason and move on. You never know what may happen in the future – life is full of wonderful opportunities.

Learning to express your emotions

Emotions can be scary because they reveal very private and personal information about who we really are. It is certainly not surprising that we have difficulty expressing our emotions at times. We are fearful that if we show our emotions, people may react in a way we find difficult to handle or we fear we may be judged unfairly when we expose ourselves.

Men in particular seem to believe that if they show emotion, it can mean that they do not seem 'manly'. When men show emotions, such as fear, sadness or anxiety, they sometimes feel inadequate. This is often because they have been conditioned and brought up to believe it is only acceptable for women to show these kinds of emotions.

But in today's society it is even becoming less acceptable for women to show their emotions, especially within the workplace. Because women have entered this once male domain, there is an expectation that they conform to male stereotypes in order to survive and thrive in the world of business. The problem is that, if revealing our emotions is not the 'done' thing, it just leaves us feeling exposed and inadequate.

So why would we want to reveal our emotions anyway? The reason is that it's healthy to release pent-up feelings. As well as giving us a sense of relief, it takes some of the weight off our shoulders. If we always hold on to our emotions then people close to us, whether partners, family or friends will never know how we feel or what we are thinking. This can lead to frustration and misunderstanding as they are always trying to guess what we are experiencing – and if they get it wrong it ends in tears. What is worse is that when we don't show our emotions, those around us often misread this as a lack of feeling, which causes hurt and fear.

If you have difficulty showing your emotions, then this will eventually have a knock-on effect on your confidence, because if you can't express yourself, then the real you is not on show. It may not affect you all the time, as you may only hold back in certain situations. Some people find that they can express themselves easily at work, but in personal relationships they can't let go. For other people it may be the opposite. Realizing when you have difficulty is the first step to solving the problem, only then you can begin to do something about it.

Fear and negativity

You may not have always been like this – just one bad experience can change the way you behave. Negative experiences stay in your mind and can become embedded until they create the fear that the same bad experience will happen again. But what are you really afraid of?

One of my clients shared a story with me about a time he cried in front of his friends. It was at a particularly low point in his life, but afterwards his friends ridiculed him to such a point that he is now afraid he will show that kind of emotion to them again. This means he is not really being himself, even when he is with his closest friends. Since having this experience, he has become excessively guarded and now finds it impossible to show how he feels to his wife and family. Events or reactions that cause us to behave in a particular way are called 'triggers'; and they are powerful catalysts for much apparently inexplicable behaviour. Once you've identified why they happen, though, you can take control again and begin to deal with them.

You need to set yourself some goals for overcoming these triggers – goals that you feel comfortable with – and then you'll find them easier to achieve. Don't try to be something or someone you're not, and don't feel you need to open up completely and express yourself to everyone. It is also healthy and wise not to expose all your emotions at once. Deal with issues in manageable blocks, not all at once. You'll only overwhelm yourself and everyone around you.

Also, avoid burdening yourself with the expectation that you're going to make a whole tranche of changes immediately. Pressure only makes things worse. Apart from anything else, it isn't supposed to be a torturous process, but one that you enjoy as you begin to experience a more relaxed and expansive you.

Always question or challenge your beliefs when working to build your confidence. Ask yourself why you think bad things will happen to you if you show your emotions, or why you think people will laugh at you if you do a presentation at work. You will find that most, if not all, of your fears are unfounded, which will probably result in your next experience being positive. The more you express yourself, the easier it will get and the more rapidly the fear will lessen and disappear. It's like anything: practise, practise, practise and it will come.

Challenge your beliefs on a regular basis. Just as you update your mobile phone, upgrade your car and clear out your cupboards, so you can review what you believe on a regular basis in order to stay fresh and clear in your thinking.

Don't leave your emotional baggage unattended!

Imagine you are in the departure lounge of an airport and are just about to fly off to your new exciting life when Confidence Airways make an announcement. At first it seems familiar, then you realize it's anything but: 'Any emotional baggage left unattended, will not be removed without warning and destroyed by us, it will just be left where it is, for you to carry around with you for the rest of your life.' Think about it – maybe you should destroy it before it destroys you.

Believe it

Now we have looked at shifting that emotional baggage, let's look at things in a slightly different light. We've been looking at how things in the past have held you back or are holding us back, like personal experiences, your childhood and your negative thoughts. Let's face it, sometimes we just don't do things because we simply don't believe we can. We have grown up with certain beliefs and they have become cemented into our psyche.

In my coaching sessions, when people are trying to discuss with me the reasons why they don't believe they have enough confidence, or why they feel they can't achieve something in their life, they often confuse reasons for excuses. They give an explanation as to why they cannot do something, believing it to be a reason. I then point out to them the possibility that it may be an excuse, and this changes their perception radically.

Often there is no basis for the reasons we give as to why we can't do something – that's because our reasons are often excuses in disguise. Our belief system tells us we can't do it, purely because we have got into the habit of thinking that way. It's a habit we have formed. We've got used to thinking this way, and have not found a way to stop.

Author Chick Moorman created a fantastic exercise called the 'I Can't' Funeral. You can either do this alone or you can get together with your friends or family to help you with it. Do whatever you feel comfortable with. Now this may feel a little odd at first, but I urge you to try it, it's simple and very effective. Every time I run this type of exercise in my workshop, people always say how powerful it is.

EXERCISE

Here are some examples of 'I can't . . .':

- I can't get a promotion at work.
- I can't be as confident as I would like to be.

- I can't seem to make friends as well as I'd like.
- I can't make my partner understand how I feel.
- I can't do a presentation in public.
- I can't lose weight.
- I can't cook.

Now write your own list of what you believe you can't do. Make sure you have written down everything you can think of, then read the list through. If you can only think of a few examples at first but know there are more, then give yourself more time.

When you have finished your list, read it through until you have memorized all the items, then tear it up. Permanently destroy the list so it cannot be read again by you or anyone else – burn it, shred it, bury it (my favourite method) or just tear it up into tiny pieces and bin it.

Once you have got rid of the paper, read the following eulogy to yourself straight away. Really take note of the words and read it more than once if you need to.

> We are gathered here today to honour the memory of 'I can't'. While he was with us on Earth he touched the lives of everyone, some more than others. In fact his name has been mentioned in every household around the world. We have provided 'I can't' with a final resting place. He is survived by his brothers and sister, 'I can', 'I will' and 'I'm going to straight away'. They are not as well known as their famous relative, and are certainly not as strong and powerful yet. But with your help they can make an even bigger mark on the world. May 'I can't' rest in peace and may everyone present pick up their lives and move forward in his absence. Amen.

Take a second or two to let the exercise sink in and have an impact on you. Reflect for a moment on what you have just done, and how symbolic the exercise is to you. You have just laid to rest all the things you think you 'can't' do. From now on, avoid using the words 'I can't', and replace them with 'I can', 'I will' and 'I am going to straight away'.

Many people find this activity symbolic, powerful and memorable. This exercise is great, as it is what we call a 'right brained' experience so it will stay in both the conscious and unconscious mind forever. To reinforce your decision, write 'I can't RIP' and add the date and pin it somewhere you will see it every day.

Other ways of releasing the past

- Clear out your wardrobes and cupboards. Throw everything away that you haven't worn for two years or more. Don't hold on to anything just in case it comes back into fashion or in case it fits you when you've lost weight. Throw away junk and anything you no longer need. This is a very cleansing process, it will clear your mind as well as your physical surroundings. If you tend to hoard things then be brave and decide to get rid of as many possessions as you can. Mementoes can turn into emotional baggage, so give them to a charity shop or other organization where they will do some good for other people. Car boot sales can be very therapeutic: you get rid of your unwanted possessions and in return make some money. Hanging on to possessions belonging to people who have left the home or passed away can hinder the grieving process. Maybe now is the time to decide to let go of them.

- Clean your house and car inside and out. Clear and clean all the surfaces and soft furnishings. Repaint walls that are drab and mend any damaged areas in your home. Organize your space so you can eliminate the build-up of clutter and keep your home and car in good order in future.

- Let go of the pressure to keep any promises you have made to people that you know you are not going to get round to fulfilling. Get away from thinking that you're going to handle everything and be a superman or superwoman. For example, if you have a friend or acquaintance who you promise to have a drink with or visit every time you speak to them on the phone, but know you won't, just stop saying it and that nagging feeling of an unfulfilled commitment will go away. Be honest with your friends, associates and yourself.

- Clear out your old address book. Contacts in your address book can become part of your 'emotional baggage'. It is great to erase details of people you know for sure you will never contact again. Remove the 'what if I need their details, just in case' anxiety from your mind. If you know you are keeping hold of an ex-partner's details with the wrong intentions, then ask yourself why you are doing this, and challenge yourself to erase it. The same goes for old work contacts, sometimes they can come in handy and sometimes they can weigh you down – only you can decide. Be brave in your decision making.

Earlier, we explored how our personality, character, confidence and attitude to life are moulded during our childhood. How often do you find yourself doing or saying something then saying to yourself: 'Oh no, that's exactly what my mother used to do!' and 'That's exactly what my father used to say.'

The older we get, the more mannerisms we recognize as those we have adopted from our parents. In fact, the more you examine your parents' behaviour the more you will come to understand yourself. Their personalities, attitudes, abilities and intelligence all have a part to play in how you are formed and who you are today.

Our behaviour patterns are formed as a result of experiences and events in our past and they still affect our ability to deal with life in the present. These are behaviour patterns we fall back on when life gets tough. In these pressure situations, elements of our character and personality come through as 'parent', 'adult' or 'child' behaviours.

If you look back over your past, you will recognize the habitual behaviour patterns you have adopted throughout your life. You can begin to separate the good from the bad. Although it is not productive to dwell too much on the past, it is useful to be able to look back and learn from it. You can acknowledge the past and then make a conscious effort to leave it behind. Take a little time to reflect on your behaviour patterns or habits that you repeat on a regular basis.

Get to know your inner self

Our confidence levels are largely the result of our thinking and attitude to life. We often feel weighed down by past experiences, stress and life in general. We are driven by two contrary forces in our lives: the personal and the public.

We experience these forces as demands on our mind, body and soul – mental health, physical health, emotional well-being and our spiritual self. The external world – work, earning money, friends, family, social expectations, cultural demands and religious beliefs – conflict with our inner need for relaxation, peace, rest and calm. Managing these conflicting demands is a constant pressure on us. As a result, we often get the balance wrong; we pay far too much attention to the external at the expense of internal. This eventually results in a lack of energy and ill health.

To avoid these pitfalls, it is vital that you learn to pay much more attention to your internal dialogue. The trouble is that it can be less vocal and less obvious than the constant – and often negative – chatter that we create for ourselves. It is this chatter that often creates pressure, which means that in some sense you are not only responsible but also in control of how you experience pressure. For some, pressure boosts confidence and provides the drive to achieve, while for others it has the reverse effect, diminishing confidence and dampening drive.

The ability to control the way you experience pressure can be very useful. Creating and channelling pressure can give you energy when you need it most. However, when you experience so much pressure that you experience anxiety, recognize it and channel it positively.

Get to know what you believe

Our opinions and beliefs are formed as a result of experience and what we are told. Beliefs are a fundamental part of what we're about, they evolve as we grow and form our character and personality. They drive us on a day-to-day basis and form the boundaries of what we do and say. The problem is that beliefs can also be very restrictive, and limit us and our potential. How many of us regularly challenge our beliefs? How often do you hear someone saying they have changed a belief?

- 'Actually, I don't believe that any more.'
- 'You know what? My views on that have changed.'
- 'You were right about what you were saying, and I was wrong.'
- 'I used to think that way, but now I'm not sure.'

Our beliefs become embedded in our mind and are habitual; our peers, society, the media and our experience of life all influence and help the development of our beliefs. If you believe, for example, that you're not good at maths you'll restrict your work – and life – options significantly. If you believe working hard is the only way to succeed, then you'll probably have to work hard to get where you want to be, whereas someone who believes work should be easy and enjoyable will have that experience. If you believe it's not worth complaining about bad service, then you'll always have to accept it without speaking out. Eventually your beliefs will damage your confidence and self-esteem, because they will prevent you from taking control and making changes. So maybe it's time you started to challenge your beliefs.

EXERCISE

Read the examples below then write down any negative beliefs you have about yourself.

- I am not a very confident person.
- I am not much fun to be around, as I don't make people laugh.
- I'm always making a fool of myself when I don't mean to.

- I don't have much to contribute to conversations.

- I am a boring person because no one asks for my advice.

- I always seem to make a mess of things – without even trying!

- I'm no good in relationships as I am a selfish person.

- I'll never be good at my job because I failed my exams.

- I'm a bad parent as I work full-time and don't spend enough time with my children.

- I'm always letting my friends down.

Now look at your list and think carefully about each point. Ask yourself: 'Do I truly believe this about myself or are they just doubts I have about myself?' There is a difference between beliefs and doubts: beliefs are deep-rooted ideas about yourself that you accept without questioning, whereas doubts are random, negative feelings you have about yourself.

Now it's time for you to work on those beliefs so you can begin to rebuild your confidence. As to the doubts, first examine them to see if you can find out where they have come from – after all, they may have developed as a result of just one incident. Each time you catch yourself having that doubt again, stop. Channel it into a positive thought to protect your self-esteem before it takes hold and develops into a belief. Eventually, you will be able to simply banish it from your thoughts.

Having recognized these negative beliefs or doubts about yourself, you are now in a position to dispel them. It is important that you do this, because these thoughts are standing in the way of you achieving greater confidence.

Look after your mental health

Next, you are going to find out more about how your brain works. Your brain is the source of your internal dialogue: it has got you where you are today and it's going to get you through life. That's why your mind needs a full service to ensure it runs efficiently. Think of your mind as a car. Imagine you're driving an old banger and the boot, back seats, passenger seat and roof rack are loaded up with boxes, cases, old furniture and junk. The engine is weighed down and can hardly get over 20 miles per hour. Smoke is pouring from the exhaust, and the engine's backfiring. Oil is leaking all over the road and you can tell that the car is about to break down at any moment. Now imagine what it would be like if this was your mind, full of emotional baggage and negative ideas, which clog up the machinery and slow everything down.

Why not drive your dream car instead? Is it a Ferrari, Porsche or a Formula One sports car? As you drive round the race track as fast as you can go, you notice the car performs like a dream. Just imagine how that would make you feel: fast, slick, lightweight and at the peak of your performance. Well, your mind can be like this if you care for it, clear out the old baggage, and do a regular service. Then you can fine-tune it into becoming that super-fast race car.

Just like the old banger, an overcrowded, highly stressed mind can break down at any time. Your mind is very precious, and yet you fill it with worry, negative thoughts and stress and don't take time to give it some tender loving care.

The mind is a complex machine and works on many levels. Sometimes it is necessary to explore deeper levels of our mind to try to understand why we feel the way we do, and why we behave the way we behave, particularly when we are feeling low in confidence. Our mind holds memories of different experiences, and these come to the surface when we are under stress or something happens to awaken them. As they come to the surface, they come into conscious awareness and this is when our unconscious mind gives us the opportunity to deal with them.

How often do you sit down, unwind your thoughts, clear your head, dump unwanted worries and banish negative thoughts? If you're like most people then not very often. For your mental health it is something you need to learn to do. Your mind needs its own form of relaxation and 'chill out' time just as much as your body. If you don't already do it, make a decision to take time to relax your mind.

Why not start today? Do some form of meditation or take time at the end of each day to deal with negative thoughts, doubts and limiting beliefs. Recognize how full your mind is of old, outdated or negative thoughts, how full of things you 'must' remember to do – maybe so full that there doesn't seem to be room for anything else? Remember that when your mind is full, it does not operate efficiently. Does your mind feel more like the old banger or more like the Ferrari? If it feels like a banger, dump your baggage so you can start driving that Ferrari.

Summary

You need to leave your past behind, deal with your emotional baggage and release negative emotions before you can begin building your confidence. Your confidence is intimately bound up with what you believe about yourself, your fears, negative thinking and limiting beliefs. But if you learn to take control of what you think and how you behave, you access your personal power, which raises your self-esteem and confidence.

Your mind is a powerful tool and learning how to use it to your advantage is key to gaining confidence. To give you an idea of how you can control your own thinking, here is an example of how one member of my family overcame his sleep problems.

My relative had always had problems sleeping. He had tried everything. But over a period of time he trained himself to control his mind until he could switch it on or off like a light switch. Now, when he goes to bed, first he gives himself time to unwind and think about what he needs to think about. Then, when he's ready to go to sleep, he mentally flicks his switch, his mind shuts down and he goes to sleep almost immediately. It's as simple as that. Before he knows it, he's asleep. He doesn't need to count sheep or read to get himself to sleep any more. This shows how you can train your mind to do things that are beneficial to you. You really can mentally dump things you don't need to think about anymore and learn to use your mind much more effectively. Are you ready to begin?

4

Don't Let It Get You Down

'Confidence is contagious, so is a lack of confidence.' – Michael O'Brien

Your alarm clock goes off: it's Monday morning. You immediately think: 'Oh no, do I really have to get up and go to work? It's Monday and I don't like Mondays, they are such stressful days at work and everyone is so miserable.' But you know you have to get up and go to work because you need to earn some money to pay the bills. So you throw back the duvet, you open the curtains and guess what? It's raining! 'That's typical,' you say to yourself. 'What a miserable day it's going to be.' You pick out some clothes from a pile on the floor, you go downstairs and see a load of post on the doormat. 'Oh no,' you say to yourself, 'not my credit card bill! Payday is ages away.' So you put the bill on a shelf in the kitchen and try to forget about it.

You go to the fridge to get out the milk to make a cup of coffee, and guess what? There isn't any. 'I don't believe it,' you moan, 'why does this always happen to me?' You realize you're running a bit late now, and you don't have time to eat breakfast, so you jump in the car. But guess what? The battery is flat. You ask your neighbour to give you a jump start. Eventually, you get on your way, battling through the morning traffic and arriving at work half an hour late. You say good morning to your colleagues, and ask how they are and they say things like: 'Knackered, I didn't sleep well last night,' and 'I've got a terrible cold,' and 'I hate Mondays!'

Now, what frame of mind do you think this is going to put you in for the rest of the day or even the rest of the week? It's only 10 am on a Monday morning and you already feel totally miserable. Do you think you'll be in a positive frame of mind or a negative frame of mind? Let's face it, you're unlikely to be feeling very upbeat or eager to take on the world, are you?

As you were reading that story, did you recognize yourself or some of the things you think. Did you say to yourself: 'That's me, I do that'? Maybe some of the things described happen to you regularly?

By allowing all those minor incidences to 'get to you' by 10 am in the morning, you are at the bottom of what I call your 'motivation ladder'. Ideally, though, you should be at the top of your motivation ladder at the start of the day. After all, you've just woken up after a night of refreshing sleep and you should be raring to go and ready to enjoy your day ahead.

We all find ourselves faced with challenges on a daily basis, some greater than others. And some people have to deal with physical, mental and social challenges as well. But the challenges I refer to here are minor ones: challenges that, in the cold light of day, are not very great. Let's take a closer look at these challenges.

Stop letting little things get to you

The weather has got to be number one on the list of time-wasting conversations and energy-wasting issues. I phoned a colleague of mine the other day, and asked her if she was having a good day. 'No,' she said, 'the weather here is terrible! It's grey, miserable and it's been raining all day.' Now, she works in an office and has a car so she doesn't even have to go out and get wet, yet the weather ruined her day. Doubtless, this same colleague will also complain when there is a period of hot, sunny weather because she's too hot and she can't work in the heat. She is a victim of the weather. I asked her why she spends so much time complaining about the weather and letting it affect her, even though she can't change it. She told me that it is a habit. She also admitted that her mood is fundamentally affected by the weather. This just proves that if you allow yourself to be affected by things you cannot change, you are likely to make yourself miserable. Will this kind of thinking make you feel more in control of your life, raise your self-esteem and help you feel more confident? Probably not.

If you think about all the everyday events that could affect your mood, you'll probably be able to see that they are all very trivial really, yet you let them get you down all the same. Running out of milk, getting bills in the post and the car not starting are hardly major events. Yet, we all allow them to cause us stress just the same. We get wound-up, angry, upset and flap until we manage to scramble our way through them. We behave as if we are the unluckiest person in the world, and that only bad things happen to us. And the result is that we end up at the bottom of our motivation ladder.

The next time you notice something small getting you down, stop yourself reacting as you usually do and instead, accept that these things are part of life and that in the great scheme of things they are very insignificant. Get things into perspective. So, the bus is late, it's raining, you've lost your keys, you've spilt red wine on your new white shirt; so what? The bus will get there eventually, it will stop raining, you can get new locks, the cleaner will rescue your shirt. Make a conscious effort not to let it get to you.

This may take some practice, but if you stay composed and focused you'll be able to get almost any event or situation into perspective. If you don't, the only person who will suffer is you, because if you don't take hold of the situation, it will take hold of you.

Think about the last traffic jam you were in or the last time you were delayed by a train or plane. All around you, people were on their way to work, going shopping, visiting friends, attending weddings, holidays, doctors appointments, meetings and so on. Imagine there were two types of people caught in the same delay. One type experiences the delay differently to the other. One type thinks: 'Oh well, there's nothing I can do about it, I'll sit calmly and wait for the traffic to move,' and comes out of the situation feeling positive, focused and in control, with normal blood pressure and ready to carry on with their day. But the second type shouts, beeps his horn, gets wound up and comes out of the situation feeling out of control, angry and exhausted. Both would have experienced the same frustrating circumstances, but one will feel physically and mentally positive and the other will feel beaten and tired.

If you get emotionally involved by every minor setback, you'll just experience a drain on your energy and end up feeling stressed and negative – and all about the most trivial things. Instead, you need to work on staying at the top of your motivation ladder. This way you'll be able to sustain a feeling of confidence and high self-esteem about yourself and the world around you. If you allow these frustrations to wash over you, you'll feel much more productive and healthy.

When I was a child, my mum told me that 'there are millions of people worse off than you so count your lucky stars'. My mum still says it today, and it is true. We moan about the rain, but those living in drought-stricken areas of the world pray daily for rain. We moan about the car battery being flat, but we should be grateful that we have a car. You know where I'm going with this one don't you? I believe you must be thankful for what you have, and let all these small and insignificant incidences go. Plough your energies into a more productive way of thinking. Perhaps you're now thinking: 'It's all very well saying it's all okay, but really, it's normal to get annoyed about these things.' Well, I don't think that's the case; it isn't normal and you do not have to react to all these minor events. After all, like the colleague whose day was made or ruined by the weather, you are only reacting to events out of habit.

Here are a few techniques to help you stay at the top of your motivation ladder. Get someone to help you with this exercise. Your helper – or even helpers – need to be people who care for you and whom you trust.

GET OUT OF THE MOANING HABIT

Every time your helper hears you moaning about something trivial, such as the weather, your workload, the cleaning, how tired you are, and so on, get them to point it out to you immediately. Do this for an agreed period of time. This will feel strange for you both at first, but it does not take long before you become so aware of it yourself so you can start to deal with it on your own.

USE MOANING TIME MORE PRODUCTIVELY

Every time you hear yourself complaining or becoming stressed about something that really is insignificant, write it down. You only need to write key words, nothing too lengthy. Count up the words at the end of the day and you will be amazed at how many times you wasted your energy on moaning about something negative. Do this for a few days and you'll find that you'll quickly start a new habit of reacting positively in any situation. Keep going for longer if you need more time to make this work.

FIND A 'HAPPY' TRIGGER

Choose a word or a phrase that you can remember easily and say it to yourself, either in your head or out loud, each time you find yourself becoming unnecessarily stressed or wound up. Here are some examples of trigger words or phrases used by some of my clients:

- 'Positive.'
- 'Stay up the ladder.'

- 'There you go again.' (Said in a humorous way.)
- 'This really is not important.'
- 'I am lucky to have what I have.'
- 'There are many more people worse off than me.'
- 'Get it into perspective.'
- 'Get a life.'
- 'Calm.'

Choose your own word or phrase. Learn it parrot-fashion as you do your PIN number, so that when you feel yourself getting stressed, you can just say it and divert your thoughts elsewhere. It's easier than you think and very effective.

Break the habit

Research shows that lack of confidence is just a habit, like becoming unfit, walking round the room in the same direction, putting your clothes away in the same place, biting your nails and so on. The way to overcome this habit is the same as overcoming any other: awareness, perseverance and practice. So all you need to do is break the old habit and form a new one.

EXERCISE

To prove to yourself what a creature of habit you are, try to think of all the things you do routinely without thinking about them, such as:

- Sleeping on the same side of the bed.
- Packing your bags with the same things when you go away.
- Buying the same food at the supermarket every week.
- Tidying your house the same way.

- Driving the same way to work.
- Washing your car every Sunday.
- Buying the same types of clothes.
- Parking in the same place.
- Going to the same restaurants.
- Playing the same games with your children.
- Writing the same types of letters to your friends.
- Visiting the same places each year.
- Eating the same food for lunch.
- Cooking the same types of meals.

The challenge now is to do things differently:

- The next time you go to the supermarket, walk round the aisles in a different direction.
- The next time you read the paper, start at a different section or read from a different direction than you normally do (i.e. back to front).
- The next time you go to a social gathering, walk into the room in a different way, for example, if you normally walk around the edge, walk straight through the middle instead.
- The next time you drive to work, choose a different route.
- The next time you go to the supermarket, buy different brands or choose foods you have never tried before.
- The next time you go out for a meal, try a different dessert, wine or main course at the restaurant.

This exercise is just a fun way of proving how we all get used to doing things in a particular way and shows how easy it is to get stuck in a routine. Notice how it feels when you do something in a different way. Does it feel odd or exciting? Does it make you feel nervous or revitalized? Have a go and see what you think.

Avoid the negatives

As you work to build your confidence it's important that you stay away from negative people. You know the ones, they're permanently miserable; their glass is always half empty rather than half full. You probably know one, or have met one, or maybe you have suddenly realized that you are one! If there was ever a time to be honest with yourself, it's now. I once heard negative types being described by a colleague as 'mood Hoovers': they zap all the positive energy out of a situation or the people around them. If you spend any amount of time in their company you will eventually feel mentally exhausted and low. In order to create a more positive environment for yourself, you need to prevent people like this bringing you down, and ultimately, you need to avoid them altogether.

Mood Hoovers are bad news. You know what happens: you go out feeling good about things, and then you meet Mr or Mrs Grumpy, and all of a sudden your mood plummets, the atmosphere changes and you get dragged down the road to negativity. Protect yourself from this from now on by maintaining your own positive state of mind.

There are ways to do this. When people start to moan or complain about something, stop them by asking at an appropriate moment: 'What good things happened to you today?' I use this all the time, and it's great fun and very effective. You'll be amazed at what some people come out with, things that you'd never have known about unless you asked. Dealing with people like this in a positive way will also help you feel upbeat and confident about yourself. Your energy levels will stay up and, even better, dedicated moaners will not bother speaking to you as much in the future so they'll be easier to avoid.

A colleague of mine once told me that his father-in-law is a 'negative'. For a period of time my colleague asked his father-in-law what good things had happened to him today, and thankfully his father-in-law stopped off-loading his moans. Of course we need to be there to support our families and friends in their times of need, but there's only so much negativity anyone can take on board. Another colleague of mine uses this analogy:

It's your day off and you are sitting in your lounge watching your favourite film on television. All of a sudden you hear the 'beep beep beep' sound of a lorry reversing, so you look out of your window and see a dumper truck reversing down your drive. It stops and suddenly it starts to tilt its load with the aim of dumping all the rubbish it has collected from the neighbourhood onto your front lawn. Would you:

a) Run to the front door, open it and shout: 'Hey, stop! What are you doing?' and run up to the driver to stop him tipping the rubbish over your lawn?

OR

b) Let the truck driver tip all the rubbish onto your lawn and not say a word?

So the question is: if you wouldn't let anyone tip rubbish onto your front lawn, why do you allow people to dump emotional rubbish onto you every day? If you are ready to take charge of what you choose to fill your head with, you have to stop people pouring negative thoughts into your mind.

> 'Negativity breeds depression and low self-esteem. Positive thinking brings motivation, excitement, interest, energy and the power to make changes.'

EXERCISE

Today, ask ten people: 'What good things happened to you today?'

Because people are more comfortable and familiar with talking about negative issues, they will probably have to think about what good things have actually happened to them.

The influence of your surroundings

So far, it's been apparent that we absorb a lot more negativity than we realize. Even if we don't want to admit it, we are influenced by our surroundings in many ways. When I was nine years old, I moved from the southeast to the northeast of Britain. Before long, I had developed a broad northern accent. When I moved back south, I lost the northern accent completely. A friend of mine was an air stewardess. She was always very image-conscious and only dressed in the smartest clothes. But when she started dating a Hell's Angel, she started to wear leather, got a tattoo and decided that washing was not for her.

Have you ever noticed how couples dress similarly and use the same phrases? We are influenced by our friends, family, the world around us, books, newspapers, television and radio; none of us is immune to our environment. A child starts school and is neat, tidy and in a perfect school uniform. Two weeks later her socks are rolled down, her jumper is tied round her waist and her school bag has been spray-painted and drawn on!

A salesman starts his job in a new company: he hasn't a bad word to say about the company, and at social gatherings he's keen to be seen to be the perfect employee, so he only drinks soft drinks. At the next social gathering, two months later, he's moaning about the workload, and his colleagues end up bundling him into a taxi and sending him home because he's had too much to drink. We soon adopt the attitudes of our close companions, even if we don't intend to and, because it's a gradual process, we barely notice.

Being influenced by our surroundings can also be a positive thing, though. Being around happy people helps us to become happy and being around inspirational people inspires us. It also means we can use our positive attitude to influence others, which in turn will help guide our life in the direction we want it to go.

If you have been spending too much time with negative people, maybe it's time to recognize this and, if you want to improve your quality of life, perhaps you need to take some action. You can spend less time around negative people by managing your time differently, and doing alternative things. In the same way, you could improve other aspects of your life. Research has proved that poor people have poor friends and rich people have rich friends; children whose parents smoke are more likely to smoke themselves; successful business people have successful business friends and so on. If you really do want to change your life, you may first have to look at who and what surrounds you so that you can start making changes that will help you along your path to success.

The influence of the media

Let's look at another key negative influence that surrounds us: the news. It's a major source of information, but the problem is that most of it is depressing and negative: bombs, disasters, wars, death, political intrigue, crime, dishonesty, economic problems etc. Just imagine how different it would be if we turned on the television and the newsreader reported upbeat stories on successes and achievements with a big grin on his or her face.

EXERCISE

When you next listen to the news, look out for positive stories. They may be shrouded in negativity and you may have to deduce a positive from a negative, but there is often a more obvious happy story in the form of '...and finally' at the end of the programme.

Although you can't change the news and how it's delivered, you can change the way you listen to it. Before you know it, you'll have an inbuilt filter that will strain out all the negative, depressing reports so you only hear the positive stuff.

Taking control and being positive

Recognizing what you can control and what you cannot will stop you wasting your time on things that you can't change. For example, campaigners learn to lobby influential people about things that they think they can change, not the things they think they can't. If you focus on the positives, you'll find that your priorities sort themselves out naturally.

I guarantee you will be happier when you have learned to think positively, in fact it will have an instant effect. If you think about things that make you laugh, you'll instantly smile and feel happy. By renewing your respect for the positives in life, by practising positive thinking and searching out the positives, you will regain an almost childlike energy and openness.

> 'A mind that has been stretched, will never return to its original dimension.' — Albert Einstein

In his book, *The 7 Habits of Highly Effective People*, Stephen R. Covey set out a simple model of where our power and influence lies; it's called the Circle of Influence.

Circle of Concern – Circle of Influence

When we look for ways to influence and change our surroundings, it is helpful to notice where we focus our time and energy. We each have a wide range of concerns, from our health, family and problems at work, to world issues, and it is these things that make up our Circle of Concern.

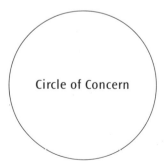

As we look at those things within our Circle of Concern, it becomes apparent that there are some things over which we have no real control and others that we can do something about. We could identify those concerns over which we have some control in a smaller area called the Circle of Influence.

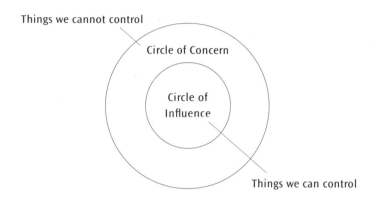

Our problems fall into three areas of influence: direct control (problems involving our own behaviour); indirect control (problems involving other people's behaviour); or no control (problems we can do nothing about, like our past or some aspect of our current situation). Confident people focus their efforts and energies on their Circle of Influence. They look at what they can change and put their energy into that. Because they are acting positively and concentrating on making a difference, they achieve more.

EXERCISE

Write down all the things that concern or worry you. Don't think too hard or edit your thoughts, just write down what comes to mind immediately. Once you have written a few things down, take a look at what you've written. Accept what you can affect or influence and what you can't affect or influence. Look at the examples below and see how yours compare.

What I can affect	What I cannot affect
My relationships with people	The weather
My workload at work	The transport system
My attitude	Future health
My career	What people think of me
My happiness	My mother-in-law!
My children and family	World economy
My confidence	Other people's actions
My outlook on life	The interest rate
My future	How my football team plays!

The exercise above contains just a few examples of what people believe they can and cannot affect – what you think you can affect may be different, for example you may believe that you can affect your health by exercising and eating healthily.

Many of us get preoccupied with our worries but most of our worries are about things we cannot affect. As a result, we are giving our focus and attention to something that we cannot directly do anything about.

Many of us worry about what other people think of us. In fact, we can become obsessed with it. By constantly guessing whether we are acceptable or not, or whether we are as good as the next person, we lose confidence, because comparing ourselves with others means we end up criticizing and finding fault with ourselves. There can be some benefit in doing this, but it is only useful to gauge your progress not to see if you 'measure up'. I'll give you an example: I enjoy playing tennis, but if I compared myself to Venus Williams, I wouldn't feel very good about myself. However, if I compared myself to someone of a similar standard then I would feel confident about my tennis-playing abilities.

I believe it is great to have an inspirational figure to look up to when you are striving to achieve something, but be careful not to expect to perform to the same standard as them when you first start out. When comparing yourself to someone else, be realistic about who it is and what it is about them that you are comparing yourself with. If you admire someone who is particularly confident then you could model yourself on them, but we are all different and what may work for one person may not work for another.

Summary

While you are admiring those inspirational people around you, you need to start taking note of all the things that are having a negative effect on you. As a reminder, here are a few everyday events that might affect you in a negative way.

- The weather.
- Traffic jams and our transport system.
- Other people's actions.
- Other people's thoughts.
- Negative people.
- The media.
- Mondays.

You now need to learn to let go of these negative triggers and put your energy into getting on with your life instead. Next time you catch yourself worrying unnecessarily about things that are out of your control, stop yourself and divert your thoughts into more productive areas that you can control.

5

Know Your Strengths

> 'The difference between can and cannot is only 3 letters, 3 letters that determine your life's direction.' – Anonymous

This is the feel-good chapter, the one where you will start to realize your own potential and where you start to feel truly confident about yourself. By the end of this chapter you will begin to know what your strengths are and what is great about yourself.

The word attitude has become a favourite with employers over the last five years. If applicants in interviews display 'the right attitude', are positive, 'hungry for the job', and will fit in with the rest of the staff, it is more appealing to employers than a long list of qualifications. The right attitude can get you everywhere, the wrong one will get you nowhere. Your attitude determines the type of world you live in. It is responsible for every success and failure you have. Think about your general attitude to things, and how it affects you at the moment.

Your attitude towards things affects how you feel about people and situations, and that in turn affects how you behave and the response you get from others. So it's actually your attitude that influences what you experience. If you approach a situation with a happy, positive and motivated attitude, you are more likely to experience a happy, positive and motivated outcome. If you approach something with a negative, pessimistic attitude, you have lost before you've started. It really can be as simple as that.

Make negativity a thing of the past

Negative attitudes come from thinking negative thoughts. And if you think the same negative thoughts over and over again, they become part of your pattern of thinking and eventually part of your personality. Your thoughts become habit, ones you probably won't even notice unless someone points them out to you. Once you develop a negative attitude you get negativity back, which means you come to expect the worst and in the end you only seem to attract failure – you become a failure magnet!

So let's look at how you can change your thinking and create a positive attitude. It might take time and effort, but then if you are creating anything great, it generally takes a bit of time and dedication. For you to start to adopt a positive attitude, you need to look at your unconscious thoughts. You need to start analysing every thought you have until positive thinking becomes a habit.

Getting from negative to positive thinking

It may not be possible to stop having negative thoughts at the click of a finger, after all, you need to replace those negative thoughts with positive ones, but you can do it with time and commitment. Some people have told me that negative situations happen to them every day and they are a reality, and have asked me why they should try to resist them? I don't entirely agree with this assertion; situations are a reality, yes, but it is your attitude towards those situations that determines whether you experience them as positive or negative. We feel like victims when bad things happen to us, yet a lot of what we experience doesn't have to feel so bad. When something happens to you which you perceive to be bad, but in reality it wasn't that bad at all, you may just have got into a habit of thinking that way, or you are being dragged down by minor occurrences or events.

The sooner you start to realize that it's you who is in control of how you think, your attitude will change. Therefore, if you take control of your attitude from now on, you can also take control of your life and your confidence levels.

When our confidence and self-esteem are low, we only see our weaknesses; if we make a mistake we take this as further proof of our shortcomings and say to ourselves: 'That just proves how stupid and useless I am.' There seems to be a natural tendency for us to bring ourselves down rather than lift ourselves up. We are taught not to 'brag' about ourselves or not to 'show off', and that the best way to behave is modestly. And as we get older, we learn that if we tell people how good we are, we risk being seen as arrogant.

Low confidence is affected by what we think of ourselves, so if we bring ourselves down, then that's exactly where we will stay – down. If we don't like ourselves or have a low opinion of ourselves, then it will be very difficult for us to feel confident. What we need is an in-built mechanism we are comfortable with, so we can build ourselves up in a way that comes across as quietly assertive rather than arrogant.

This exercise is called the strengths survey. It will have a great impact on you, as it will help you get you in touch with what you are good at. It is best completed when you're feeling confident, upbeat and really good about yourself. You need to ask a close family member or friend to complete the strengths survey for you. What they have to do is write a list of your best qualities. The person you ask should know you well, and be able to be honest when giving you their feedback. The exercise will only take a few minutes and will make you feel great.

Once your partner has created a list of your strengths, ask them to talk through their answers with you so you are clear about what they mean. They may like to share the reasons why they have put a particular strength down, as some may surprise you. Listen intently and take note of what they say so you can really take it on board. You will feel great once they have shared their thoughts with you.

Keep the answers somewhere safe, and refer to them whenever you are feeling down or low in confidence. Review it whenever you need to raise your confidence and feel really positive and special – because you are. Allow yourself to feel good about yourself and proud of who you are. I know a company director who keeps his strengths survey results in his wallet, and anytime he feels like a confidence boost he reads it. I also read about an army soldier who carried a similar list in his backpack when he went off to war. It reminded him of why he was such an amazing husband and father so whenever he was feeling low, he read the list to give himself a boost.

You can do this exercise more than once: why not ask different sets of people you know to do it to get an all-round view of your strengths? You'll not only get several sets of strengths to boost you, you'll also learn a lot about yourself. So, why not ask your family, your friends and maybe your manager or colleagues at work for their feedback (if that's appropriate and comfortable for you).

Do the strengths survey with a group as part of a team-building exercise. First, make sure you know each other well enough to be able to give positive feedback. Next, ask everyone to write their name at the top of a sheet of paper then to fold it in half so the name can't be seen. Next, shuffle up the sheets of paper, and hand each member of the group one of the sheets. If someone gets their own name, they should return it and take another one. Each person then writes down all the great things they can think of about the person on their sheet. Keep going until everyone has written something on each sheet of paper (except their own, of course). Add more sheets if you run out of space.

EXAMPLES OF STRENGTHS YOU COULD LIST:

Great dress sense, wonderful entertainer, good friend, very funny, intelligent, very caring, smart, successful in business, great parent, great mentor, great role model, fabulous party host, very creative … and so on.

We can be friends with people for years and never get round to telling them how much we value them. The next time you speak to your friends or family don't forget to tell them how great you think they are. You will make their day and make yourself feel great too.

List your achievements

Another way of making yourself feel good is to take time out to look at what you've achieved in your life. I often find that if you ask people what they have achieved, they hesitate for a while and then say: 'Not much. Got a job, bought a car, that's about it.' That's rarely all there is to someone's achievements, but because we fear appearing arrogant, we often play down what we've done. When we assess our lives, we only think of the big, obvious achievements and tend to undervalue other things we have done, like overcoming a fear or making a change.

Take a minute to think of everything you have achieved in your life so far. Remember that you have probably achieved much more than you normally give yourself credit for so there will be many achievements you can add to your list. Prove it to yourself by completing the exercise below.

This exercise is called 'Splitting Your Life into Thirds'. Using the layout in the example below, list all your achievements in each third of your life.

0–15 years	15–30 years	30– 45 years
Learned to smile	Learned to kiss!	Had my daughter
Learned to walk	Learned to drive	Learned Spanish
Learned to talk	Learned about alcohol!	Learned to garden
Learned to ride a bike	Learned about love	Learned about computers
Learned to make friends	Learned to cook	Travelled
Learned to spell	Travelled	Still learning to dance!
Learned to read	Passed my exams	Bought my dream car
Learned to write	Gained my qualifications	Bought my first house
Learned to sing (badly)	My first holiday alone	Got married
Learned to add up	My first flat	Learned to play chess
Learned my times tables	Bought my first car	Won my works incentive
Learned sports	Learned the guitar	Made new friends

Don't take any of your achievements for granted – you are amazing so don't forget it. Hang onto the list and read it whenever you want to boost your confidence.

The attitude of gratitude

Appreciating what you have will improve your self-esteem and confidence enormously. Take a look at your list and think about how lucky you are to have achieved so much. It's easy to take things for granted, but there are many people who are much worse off than we are. I always think about that when I'm challenged by something. Appreciating what you have is an excellent way of focusing your mind on the positives in your life, both consciously and unconsciously. As a society, we rarely think that what we have is enough. If we have good health, we take it for granted. If we have a decent income, we moan about how little we have left at the end of each month. If we have beautiful children, we moan about how much work they are. If we have a house, we always want a bigger and better one. I certainly think it's healthy to have ambitions and goals, and to want to better yourself, but it's important to celebrate what you have, too. This way you'll get more out of it.

There is a theory that what we focus on expands. This means we can influence what we attract into out lives by giving our attention to it. Unfortunately, we are conditioned to focus on the negative side of life, so if five great things and one bad thing happens to us, we're more likely to focus on the bad thing. Before you develop your confidence any further, you need to get into the habit of thinking positively and you can do this with positive affirmations.

Positive affirmations

You're probably familiar with positive affirmations. They're a really effective method of reversing negative beliefs. Using affirmations allows you to select a thought, and plant it into your unconscious, so that you feel good about yourself.

'An affirmation is a positive thought that you repeat to yourself.'

Affirmations can feel strange when you first start using them, but they are really effective once you get used to them. The theory is that frequently repeated phrases influence the unconscious mind. If you think about your childhood, you can probably remember things your parents repeated over and over again, mostly to instill habits in you, for example, cleaning your teeth.

Repeating positive phrases or affirmations can reverse the negativity 'tape' that often plays in our minds all day. It is not necessarily essential that you believe the words you use to start with, because it is only by repeating your own affirmations that you start to believe them. It takes some will-power to practise this and you'll no doubt hear a little voice in your head saying: 'You don't believe that do you?' or 'You know you feel terrible, so don't kid yourself.' But soon these thoughts will be drowned out by your positive affirmations. There are a couple of points you need to consider before creating an affirmation.

First, you must avoid affirmations that include negatives like: 'I won't fall out with my girlfriend' or 'I won't eat chocolate.' You won't get the desired result because your mind can't process a negative and so what it will hear instead is 'eat chocolate', and 'fall out with my girlfriend', hence you'll want to eat chocolate even more and you'll argue with your girlfriend – exactly what you didn't want. It is better to phrase it in a way that is more positive, for example, 'I will eat more healthily,' and 'I will take more care over my relationship.'

If you think back to your school days, and when you were given lines to write, you'll probably recall that they were designed to remind you what not to do. For example, 'I mustn't forget my homework' and 'I mustn't talk in class.' These are in the negative so if you think about it, they were actually encouraging you to do what you shouldn't. Your unconscious mind was hearing 'I must forget my homework' and 'I must talk in class!'

The second thing to remember when creating them, is that affirmations are much more powerful when you write them down or say them out loud. This is because it helps you stay more focused on what you want to achieve. If you just think your affirmations, then other thoughts can get in the way like: 'I wonder what I'll have for tea' or 'I wonder what the football score is.' Saying them out loud or writing them uses more of your senses and so will have a more powerful effect. Repetition is the key to affirmations, you are trying to replace your existing belief system with a new one so you'll need to persevere. Don't expect to say, 'I am very confident' ten times and change your belief instantly.

Below are some examples of affirmations that will help build your confidence. Read them through and see which ones resonate with you. Repeat your chosen affirmation at least 20 times each day for the next two or three weeks and see what happens. A good time to do this is in the morning when you wake up or just before you go to sleep – or maybe both. This way you'll start or end the day with positive thoughts.

- If competing in a sport:
  'I will play a good game and win.'
- If presenting at work:
  'I will give a great presentation and everyone will be impressed.'
- If going for an interview:
  'I will do my very best to secure the job.'
- If meeting new people:
  'I am interesting, kind and great fun.'
- If dealing with a tense situation:
  'I can resolve this quite easily.'

Our words influence how we feel and what we believe and this, in turn, affects what we say and how we feel – use this to your advantage and make it a productive circle.

> 'The greatest revolution of our generation is the discovery that human beings, by changing the inner attitudes of their minds, can change the outer aspects of their lives.'
> — William James, psychologist and philosopher

Symbols of your success

From now on, make a commitment to yourself to keep an ongoing record of your strengths and achievements. It will really help you maintain your confidence because you will be focusing your attention on all the things you are good at rather than constantly bringing yourself down.

Surround yourself with possessions or objects that make you feel good about yourself. Carry around photographs of your children, friends or family, as these relationships are representations of your achievements just like anything else.

Make sure you have pictures around your house of all the people who mean a lot to you. A friend of mine has pictures in his office and at home, which represent his goals and dreams. It may be a picture of a car or a yacht he wants to buy, a house he ultimately dreams of living in, a country he wants to visit or anything else that reminds him of what he wants to achieve. He displays his certificates for qualifications he has achieved and trophies he has won from sport. He has letters – anything from a loving letter from his mother to a special letter from a friend – framed, because they make him feel good. You may think that all this sounds a bit over-indulgent, but it makes him feel good and reminds him that he is an achiever. It gives him the confidence and motivation to keep pursuing his dreams.

A friend of mine keeps a success or victory log – a small notebook where she writes down all her achievements in life. Why not do the same. You can carry it around with you and add to it when you achieve something new, however small you may think it is. Like the strengths survey, it will give you an instant boost.

How often do you congratulate people you know on their achievements? Do you tell those close to you and maybe not so close to you how proud of them you are? A very good friend of mine recently came to stay with me. He spent some time with my family and commented on how delightful he thought my daughter is, and that he hoped his daughter would grow up to be as delightful as her. That compliment really touched me and made me feel very proud, not only of my daughter, but also of the influence I had had on the way she is growing up and the person she is becoming. His words have stayed with me and probably always will.

We tend to remember when someone says lovely things to us – partly because it doesn't happen very often and partly because it makes us feel good. Give more compliments to those people who matter to you, as not only will you make them feel good but you will make yourself feel good too. Our self-image determines how we feel about ourselves and what we think of ourselves. If we maintain a good self-image then we will be able to focus our minds on the successes we have had and the compliments that people have paid us. Having a positive self-image does not mean being arrogant or conceited. A healthy self-image or self-love allows us to develop respect for ourselves and for those around us.

A healthy self-image will help us accept compliments gracefully too. If you were to congratulate the golfer Tiger Woods on winning a tournament, he wouldn't say it was just luck or that it was only because the other players had a bad day, he would just say: 'Thank You.' If you complimented Madonna on a great new album, she wouldn't say she wasn't sure if it was good enough or ask you if you think people will like it, she would say: 'Thank you very much, I like it too.' Successful people know the value of their own ability and have a sense of their own worth. After all, it's difficult to attain that level of success without believing in your own ability.

A compliment should be given and accepted like a gift. It takes thought and effort. Make sure when you receive a compliment that you receive it with grace and use it to make yourself feel good. Imagine if an associate of yours remarked on how great you were looking, and you replied: 'I think I look fat in this outfit.' You will then feel uncomfortable for not being able to accept the compliment in the spirit in which it was given, and your associate will feel just as awkward for giving it. They'll also remember you as someone who cannot accept compliments, who is insecure about their appearance and who thinks they look fat.

It is true that if you work at making others around you feel good then it will rub off on you. It's a bit like when you get older and you learn that giving gifts is more rewarding than receiving them because you gain pleasure from making others happy. Giving compliments is like giving gifts, so give one today and start feeling great.

EXERCISE

Show more appreciation of the people around you and notice their successes. If you are someone who doesn't give compliments often, but would like to, decide to give one a day. Share your feelings with those close to you and make their day.

Focus your thoughts on what you are good at to give yourself an instant confidence boost. It automatically puts you in a positive frame of mind; one that will support you in anything you want to do. It will instantly make you feel good about yourself. This is essential when building your confidence as your thoughts affect how you feel.

Summary

We need to get to know exactly what our strengths are so we can focus on them. Knowing what they are will make you feel good about yourself, which in turn will help you to feel more confident about yourself and your abilities. Surround yourself with reminders of all that you have achieved and find pictures or objects that remind you of your goals and the important things you want from life.

Understand and celebrate all that you have achieved in your life, and, as the exercise on page 89 shows, when you split your life into thirds, you will have achieved so much more than you give yourself credit for, in fact much more than you can remember or currently acknowledge.

Showing appreciation for others is an excellent way of focusing your mind on the positives in our lives. Positive affirmations can also be used as a way of reversing your negative thoughts about yourself. Remember, an affirmation is a positive thought that you repeat to yourself. Using affirmations may feel strange at first, but it allows you to select a thought, and plant it into your unconscious, so that you can feel good about yourself and build your confidence.

Remember too that if you give compliments you are more likely to receive them and that when you do get a compliment, you make sure you accept it with grace. Really listen to what is being said to you and take it on board, because you have earned it. Enjoy the compliments and you'll attract more!

Your Thoughts and How You Feel

'If you think you can or you think you can't, you're right.' — Henry Ford, industrialist

Confidence comes from within and is built on what and how we think. If you think positively about yourself, you will raise your confidence. If your thoughts up until now have been negative, it means you need to become aware of what you're thinking at all times so you can change your negatives into positives. Our thoughts come to us in the form of internal chatter. This chatter can have a dramatic effect on how you feel and often it's critical or negative.

Negative thinking is a habit that has formed over a long period. No one is born negative or insecure; self-doubt, low self-esteem and lack of confidence are learned and developed through negative thinking. So what is negative thinking? It's simply a series of repeated thoughts that we have taken seriously and come to believe. If you had never learned to believe your negative thoughts, then you wouldn't have learned to have low confidence and poor self-esteem.

The good news is that only you are responsible for your negative thoughts, which means you can change them. If you can learn to put aside the negative thoughts you have about yourself, then you can also learn to reverse them and begin to believe something positive instead.

So, the real key to gaining higher confidence levels and increasing your self-esteem lies in thinking positive thoughts. We all talk to ourselves and we all have internal chatter – in fact psychologists believe we have about 50,000 thoughts a day and they're mainly about ourselves – but it is the nature of that chatter that determines much of our experience of life. Our thoughts contain information and feedback that we give to ourselves about our own performance and ability. Think for a moment about the sorts of things you say to yourself. If you find this difficult then make an effort to become more aware of your thoughts over the next few days, and notice when they are positive and when they are negative.

Here are a few examples of some of the thousands of negative thoughts that my clients have shared with me. See if you recognize any of these thoughts as being similar to your own:

- I've got those huge bills to pay at the end of the month, I can't do it.
- I haven't called my friends for ages, they'll think I'm a rubbish friend.
- I'm broke; in fact I never have any money.
- My car needs fixing and I just know I can't afford it.
- The weather's awful; it's never nice on my days off.
- I'm fat and can't lose weight.

- I'm looking old and wrinkled.
- I don't play with my kids enough as I'm too tired.
- I can't afford a holiday this year as my mortgage has gone up.
- Why can't I go out more often with my friends?
- This job's boring but I'm not clever enough to get a promotion or change my job.
- I'm always tired and don't have the energy to enjoy life.
- My partner and I never have any quality time together any more.

If we have over 50,000 thoughts in a day and most of them are negative, think about the impact this is likely to have over a long period. No wonder we feel miserable, insecure and lacking in confidence so much of the time.

Get to know your internal dialogue

To raise your confidence levels and feel better about yourself, you need to learn to control your internal dialogue and replace negative thoughts with positive ones. When lying awake at night in bed, most of us let our minds wander aimlessly. When we 'think things through', we're assessing how our day has gone, planning what we need to do tomorrow, and worrying about what we haven't done today. The trouble is that with all these thoughts running though our heads so late at night, we are likely to fall asleep feeling negative and down, rather than contented and smiling. Be aware of what thoughts you have just before you go to sleep tonight.

I'm sure you can recall waking up from a really happy dream and wanting to get straight back to sleep in order to return to the dream because it made you feel good. If you learn to change your internal dialogue, you can recreate that feeling when you are awake too. So rather than lying in bed worrying, why not use that time in a more productive way by thinking positive thoughts and feeling good about yourself.

If you take control of your thoughts, you'll begin to affect the course of your internal dialogue and, in turn, how you feel. To take control of this chatter, it is useful to write down some of your repetitive negative thoughts so you can see them for what they are – aimless ramblings.

The words you use to express your feelings to yourself have a significant affect on their power. For example, if you say to yourself: 'I didn't sleep a wink last night,' you'll feel even more tired than if you just say: 'I didn't sleep very well.' It's important to describe your feelings as accurately as you can and not to over-dramatize the situation. This way, you will retain a sense of being under control and keep things that happen to you in proportion. Exaggerating events, ignoring positives and creating 'all or nothing' thinking will effect how you feel, what you experience and what you remember about events.

> 'A pessimist sees the difficulty in every opportunity, an optimist sees the opportunity in every difficulty.'
> – Sir Winston Churchill, British Prime Minister (1940–1945)

Challenging your thoughts

The diagram below shows the cycle you get into when you acquire the habit of thinking negatively.

1. You experience negative thoughts about your performance.

4. Your performance is affected.

2. You start to experience feelings of anxiety.

3. Your body responds with an adrenalin rush.

Can you see that negative thinking becomes a vicious circle driven by your own initial negative thought? Your thoughts affect your feelings, your feelings affect your performance and your poor performance affects your confidence. Your low confidence then affects your thoughts, and so on.

EXERCISE

How can you tell how much of your own thinking is negative rather than positive? This exercise will answer that question. Sit comfortably in a chair or lie down on the bed. Make sure that you will not be disturbed. Clear your mind of anything you are worried about and simply pay attention to the thoughts that come into your mind. Do this for at least five minutes or longer if possible.

Start paying attention to what you are thinking at other moments as well, for example, when you are in the bath or shower, on the tube, bus or train and maybe while you are doing the dishes or brushing your teeth. You will be surprised at how often negative thoughts come into your mind.

Look at the list below and see how many of the thought patterns set down here are familiar to you:

- Things that may happen.
- Things that may not happen.
- Things that should happen.
- Things that should not happen.
- Things that did happen.
- Things that did not happen.
- Things you should have said.
- Things you should not have said.
- Things that you wish would happen.
- Things that you wish had not happened.

- Things that people said.
- Things that people did not say.
- Things that your boss has said.
- Things that your boss has not said.
- Things you do not like.

And so on . . .

I don't know about you, but I find it tiring just reading that list, let alone thinking it. Of course, I'm not suggesting that it's never appropriate to think negatively about things; after all, sometimes it may be necessary to think that way; letting off steam occasionally and having the odd moan obviously isn't going to do you much harm. But many people spend a massive amount of time locked in these negative thought patterns. The list demonstrates how much there is to occupy your internal dialogue. Amazingly it goes unnoticed most of the time because it is so familiar to us.

Many, if not all, of us have conversations with ourselves in our heads ... which is fine when they're positive. Unfortunately, most are negative and are therefore not good for us. If you can become conscious and fully aware that you are engaged in these mental conversations with yourself, you can begin to take control of them and direct them into positive thoughts. Best of all, you can start to dismiss negative thoughts that affect your confidence. This is a powerful technique and a key aspect of your quest to become a more confident and happy person. Everyone I worked with who learned this technique said it was invaluable in helping them become confident and happy.

When negative thoughts come into your mind, drop them like hot cakes. Or if that's too abrupt for you, imagine them floating away like leaves on the wind. Whatever you do, stop giving them the attention you are used to giving them. To remove the power from that negative internal voice, why not imagine a voice that makes you laugh, for example, Donald Duck's or Homer Simpson's. It will radically reduce the impact of the negative or critical thought. When you replace that negative thought with a positive, encouraging one, why not use a sexy, or inspirational voice. What about Barry White's or Martin Luther King's? As soon as you start to take control of your thoughts you will feel liberated because you will be in a position to channel your energies where you want them to go.

Making positive thinking work for you

If you are a pessimist or feeling down, it may take a little longer to experience the effects of positive thinking. For example, if you say to yourself: 'I am feeling very happy', and you don't instantly feel good, you might find your next thought is: 'There you go, I had a positive thought, so why don't I feel happy?' There are a couple of factors to consider.

Take a look at the thought that followed the positive one, it was a sceptical one, wasn't it? What happened was that your habit of negative thinking kicked in before you had a chance to really benefit from the positive thought. But don't worry, just give yourself time to get to grips with the new way of thinking and keep practising.

The second reason why positive thinking might not have an instant impact on you is that you have built up a resistance to positive thoughts. It's like being deprived of compliments for so long that when you get one, you don't know how to respond or receive it.

Of course, the likelihood that just one thought will instantly impact on you is less than if you have a lot of similar thoughts. Around 80 per cent of what we think each day is negative, so our minds need to be repaired and healed from the battering they have already taken before the new thinking can take effect. So just by changing one negative thought into a positive one might not do it. But changing 40,000 negative thoughts into positive ones will have a huge impact on your confidence.

Why not set a goal for yourself and see if you can eliminate as close to 100 per cent of those negative thoughts as you can? The nearer to 100 per cent you get the more positive you will feel and, in turn, this will give you the confidence you crave.

Review your thoughts regularly to monitor whether they are positive or negative. Research shows that it takes three weeks to replace an old habit with a new one, and another nine weeks to turn that new behaviour into a new habit. So get started, and before you know it you will be an automatic positive thinker.

EXERCISE

Here are two really simple and effective ways to tackle your negative thinking.

1. Ask a good friend, trustworthy colleague or partner to monitor what you say for at least two days. Ask them to interrupt you and tell you every time you start saying something negative. This may be hard at first, but it doesn't have to be embarrassing or frustrating, it can be fun – and it's a real eye-opener.

2. Draw a positive image (you decide what it is) on a piece of card or buy a greetings card that you like, then put it somewhere prominent to remind yourself to think positively.

Initially, switching to positive thinking is like setting an alarm clock to wake you up in the morning. It only becomes automatic if you keep doing it. It's like preparing your mind for the day ahead: if you don't focus on your work, your mind will wander to other things, such as food, friends, bills and worries! The mind needs self-discipline in order to be positive, just as it needs order to focus. Like any other type of focus and effort, it requires discipline and practice. Unfortunately, for most people this is not as simple as saying: 'That's it, from now on I'm going to be positive.' I read somewhere that it's like working in the positive shop – you have to go in each day and take something off the shelf. However, it is never dull or uneventful, it can be a very exciting place. Anything learned in the positive shop makes you want to learn more.

What positive thinking gives you

The first thing you'll probably notice when you start focusing on positive thoughts is that you'll instantly feel better and more excited about life. You'll probably also notice that the world seems a much more exciting, brighter and bigger place. You may also start to see new possibilities, feel new hope and find answers to your problems. You could discover fun where there was boredom, friends where you had acquaintances and knowledge where you thought there was nothing more to be learned.

Looking on the bright side will alter your priorities, you'll become less tolerant of negative people and you may want to make new, more positive friends. And things that used to drag you down may not bother you any more.

EXERCISE

Just to prove to you that positive thinking can have an almost immediate effect on how you feel, read the following list and remember when you last did each thing. If you've never done it, imagine what it would be like to experience it. There are 20 things listed here, but I am sure you can think of many more examples.

- Laughed so much your mouth ached.
- Fell in love.
- Heard your favourite song on the radio.
- Laughed out loud.
- Laid on the beach.
- Made new friends and spent time with old ones.
- Woke up and realized you still have a few hours left to sleep.
- Had a hot shower or bath.
- Watched the sun set or rise.

- Made a long distance phone call.
- Had someone tell you how beautiful or handsome you are.
- Giggled at a personal joke.
- Had a good dream.
- Received an admiring glance from a stranger.
- Found money in an old coat.
- Won a really competitive game.
- Enjoyed your favourite drink.
- Watched someone open a much-wanted present you had given them.
- Heard friends laugh.
- Ordered your favourite take-away when you are hungry.

Just thinking about these things will bring a smile to your face and give you a warm feeling inside. Use happy and special thoughts like these when your confidence takes a knock or you feel low.

EXERCISE

As we get older, our memories can fade, which is why it is important to keep our minds active. Make a list, like the one above, of all your happy memories, and carry them around with you. Whenever you are feeling low or need a boost, read your list and it will give you an instant high – that will definitely put a smile on your face.

Smile and the world smiles with you

Talking of putting a smile on your face, there's nothing like humour to lift your spirits. When you laugh, endorphins are released in your brain giving you a natural high, which in turn makes you feel great. Laughing also exercises your lungs and, in some cases, relieves pain. You can only really laugh when you are feeling comfortable and relaxed, and, of course, relaxation is good for the body and mind in itself. All these positive emotions are wonderful tonics to help you to build your confidence. Whatever makes you laugh, commit to doing more of it. You can't tremble with nerves and laugh at the same time, so you have to choose – which will it be? Laughing will help you stay healthy, and the healthier you feel, the more confident you will feel.

The next time you are about to go into a situation where you are feeling nervous or unsure of yourself, rather than adding to your pain by feeling unhappy about it, smile and think funny thoughts to put yourself at ease. As you relax, you'll start to feel more confident. Of course, if that seems too difficult, you could just fall back on the old trick of imagining the group of people or person you are about to meet, naked or on the toilet. That will put a smile on your face, but make sure you don't laugh out loud; it may be a little awkward to explain the joke!

EXERCISE

Take some time out to plan how you are going to laugh more. Here are some examples of things you can do. While they are all fairly obvious, if you write them down, it will remind you what to do and help you think of your own ideas.

- Watch a funny film.
- Read a funny book.
- Go to a comedy club.
- Read your old joke book.
- Make a 'funny memories' list or a mini diary featuring all the funny moments you can recall.
- Get together with friends who are fun to be with.
- Play board games that make you laugh.
- Look back through old photo albums.
- Watch your favourite cartoons.

Now take some time to plan when you are going to indulge in your 'laughter' activities, and make sure you get a dose regularly.

Other people's negatives

How often do you observe what is going on around you, and in particular what is being said? You can tell a lot about people from the words they use. Listen to how many negative phrases other people use, and this will give you an indication of how they think.

There is probably someone where you work that you dread talking to you because they are the office 'neg'. All they seem to do is moan about the weather, working conditions, lack of holiday and so on. You know instantly that they are negative thinkers from what they say. Take some time out to observe other people in action and see if you can spot the negative thinker amongst them.

Whilst you are taking some time to observe others, also look at their facial expressions. These can also reveal what people are thinking. How many times have you seen someone sitting opposite you on the train start grinning to themselves. If they are not reading anything, it must be what they are thinking that makes them smile. It shows how powerful thoughts can be, even though they are invisible.

Summary

Our thoughts affect our mood and how we feel about ourselves – and this affects our confidence. It turns into a downward spiral where the lack of confidence restricts what we do and say. When we perceive that we have failed or done badly, we start the critical self-talk with more energy and this reduces our confidence.

The only effective way to turn around this situation is to change your thought processes. Tune into your inner chatter, adjust the voice and change the words. It sounds easy and to some extent it is, but it takes perseverance and tenacity to see it through. But like the negative spiral, the positive one is powerful, too. Once your belief system kicks in, you won't have to make an effort to feel positive about yourself, you just will. It only takes a few weeks to turn things around. That isn't long. To help the process, focus on what you do want, rather than what you want to avoid. This way, you'll attract positive events and this will support your positive self-talk further.

You can do it, and you and your confidence are worth the effort. If you treat it like a game and are light-hearted with yourself, it will be easier to keep going. So why not start today?

'Nurture your mind with great thoughts.'
— Benjamin Disraeli, British statesman

7

It's Your Choice

'Look for your choices, pick the best one and go with it.' – Anonymous

Things happen in life and it's a fact that we cannot control a lot of them, but I don't think there's any point in worrying about them either. Worrying gets you nowhere. If you focus on your Circle of Influence (see page 80), put your energies into things you can affect and control, and ignore the things you can't, you will start to re-programme your mind to think differently. When you understand that you are in control of your thoughts and your feelings, you will have the freedom to choose to be confident.

We tend to blame others and the world in general for what happens to us and how we feel. It's not unusual to hear people saying: 'You made me feel really unhappy when you did that.' What's wrong with saying something like that? After all, it's a fairly normal thing to think and you've probably said it yourself at some time or other. But I believe that only you can make yourself feel a particular way.

Most of us go through life letting other people's actions and words affect us deeply. I expect you can remember a criticism made of you by someone close, in fact, you can probably recite it word for word. But if you think about it, it was you who created the feeling (in response to the words), not the person who said the words.

> 'No one can make me feel inferior without my consent.'
> — Eleanor Roosevelt

That's right, no one can make you feel anything you don't choose to feel. 'Oh, come on!', I can hear you thinking. 'It's impossible to be so confident that nothing affects you.' Well perhaps. After all, I know that if my mother makes a comment or criticizes me I find it difficult not to take it to heart, because her opinion matters to me. But what I have learned to do is choose how I respond in certain situations.

You may find your emotions and reactions difficult to control at times, particularly when they are connected to situations or people very close to you. But you can learn to control them and understand them. And by learning to do this you will become stronger by increasing your confidence in yourself.

Let me give you an example. If someone you didn't know came up to you and said: 'You know what, I think you're an idiot', you could react on one of two ways. First, you could think: 'Oh no! How did they find out?', or you could think: 'Hang on, they don't even know me, why should I take any notice of their opinion? I know I'm not an idiot.' What would the impact be of these two reactions to the same event? If you take the first option, you'll end up feeling low about yourself, even if what was said wasn't true. Whereas if you take the second option then your self-esteem and confidence will not be affected by the event and you'll be untouched by the criticism.

How events affect our confidence

$$E + R = O$$
$$E = EVENTS \quad R = REACTION \quad O = OUTCOME$$

Which means: Events + Reaction = Outcome.

The events in your life and your reaction to them will result in an outcome. In other words you are in control of the end result in many situations in your life. Give this formula some thought. Here are some examples to consider.

1 Being stuck in a traffic jam

Reaction 1
Event = Traffic jam
Reaction = Lose temper
Outcome = Feel stressed, hot and bothered, can't think straight

Reaction 2
Event = Traffic jam
Reaction = Stay calm
Outcome = Remain focused, feeling okay, thinking clearly

2 Your partner is late meeting you

Reaction 1
Event = Boyfriend/girlfriend/partner is late meeting you
Reaction = Lose your temper and have an argument
Outcome = Evening ruined, not talking to each other, you feel terrible

Reaction 2
Event = Boyfriend/girlfriend/partner late
Reaction = Remain calm, they apologize, talk normally
Outcome = Communication, good evening, you feel fine

3 Your boss overloads you with work

Reaction 1
Event = Boss piles loads of work onto you
Reaction = Feel very stressed, unfocused, begin to panic
Outcome = Unproductive, feel ill, little achieved,
    unhappy boss

Reaction 2
Event = Boss piles loads of work onto you
Reaction = Stay focused, discuss priorities with boss, or delegate
Outcome = Productive, respect from boss, workload managed

4 You don't get that job

Reaction 1
Event = Unsuccessful job interview
Reaction = Negative thoughts, think you are no good, lose
    confidence
Outcome = Low self-esteem, very low confidence, bad
    experience

Reaction 2
Event = Unsuccessful job interview
Reaction = Rational thoughts, evaluate performance, learn from
    interview
Outcome = Learn from experience, increase chance of future
    success, high self-esteem

You see, you really do have a choice about how you feel because you can decide how you react to certain events in your life.

There is a more extreme example, which proves that being in control of your reactions can help you through some of the most difficult times in your life. When people who lose someone close to them choose to accept their loss and carry on with their life, their experience of the loss becomes something they can cope with and move on from. People who don't choose to accept the loss, often mourn more deeply and for a longer period of time, which means it takes longer to move on and cope with the loss.

Time to change a reaction

When an event happens, we usually only have a split second or two to decide how to react. For example, if your partner was late meeting you, you might react with anger rather than reason. If you are caught in a traffic jam, you might feel instant anger or seethe with frustration at the situation.

But we have time to decide how to react and if we decide to be rational, we can train ourselves to think about things a little longer before just reacting. Apart from anything else, our reactions are just habits, which means we can learn new ones.

EXERCISE

Write down all the situations or reasons you know of that tend to cause you to react negatively or, as a client of mine once put it: 'Fire off without thinking'. The list below will give you some starting points.

- You are asked to do a presentation at work, you become instantly nervous and start to dread the event.
- There is office gossip about you and you instantly feel victimized and depressed by the fact that people are talking about you.
- Your children criticize you and you immediately take it to heart.
- Your boss says your work needs to improve and you instantly become paranoid that you are going to be fired.
- Your partner says you are no fun any more and you feel instantly hurt by their comment.

These examples show how easy it is to react and make ourselves feel low when we don't take the time to rationalize the situation. All the situations above happen daily to millions of people, which just means there are millions of people feeling low in confidence right now because they take on board the comments and criticisms of others and make themselves feel that way.

However, if you decide to take control and choose how to react and how to feel about what happens, the next time someone criticizes you, you can tell yourself it is only their opinion. When you next find yourself delayed or in a traffic jam, you can decide to accept the circumstances and stay calm. The next time you find yourself in any of these or similar situations, take a breath, pause and think about how you want to react so you can affect your outcome.

Life is a long series of choices and decisions; every day we are faced with choices about what to eat, where to go, who to talk to, what to say to people (and ourselves), how we can react and so on. The decisions we take largely determine how we feel. Look at the chart below to see how an everyday decisions could affect you either positively or negatively.

Possible positive outcome	Possible negative outcome
Choose to let go	Choose to hang on
Choose to say it's okay	Choose to say it's not okay
Choose not to dwell on issues	Choose to dwell on issues
Choose forgiveness	Choose anger
Choose to think it's fine to disagree	Choose the need to prove you're right
Choose not to take it personally	Choose to take it personally
Choose not to get so deeply into it	Choose to find out the facts
Choose to see the good things in it	Choose to look for the faults
Choose to appreciate the thought	Choose to be disappointed at the thought
Choose to think it will be me some day	Choose to think 'why can't it be me?'
Choose to feel happy for others	Choose to feel others have all the luck
Choose to think 'that's life'	Choose to think 'it's not fair'
Choose not to think too hard about it	Choose to over-analyse It

EXERCISE

Consider how you currently choose to respond to certain events in your life. Write down all the examples you can think of where you could choose to react differently. Keep the list to hand, so you can add to it over the next few weeks. Take a look at the examples below.

The Event	How I currently react	How I could choose to react next time
Being caught in a traffic jam	Get wound up and feel stressed	Accept the situation and keep calm
My partner doesn't call me when they say they will	Feel upset and have a row with him/her	Stay calm and focus my mind on other things
My boss is rude to me	Feel angry and upset	Put his behaviour down to him having a bad day
It's raining for my summer barbeque	Feel upset, angry and think I'm not going to enjoy myself	Enjoy the barbeque – you can't control the weather and there are worse things that could have happened
I'm asked to make a presentation at a meeting	Feel sick, get nervous and am not able to concentrate at work	Be flattered that I'm asked and don't worry about what other people may think about me
I am not invited out with a group of friends	Feel upset and take it personally	Accept what has happened, make sure you have not upset them and don't dwell on it as it's not worth worrying about

When making choices about how to react, the hardest thing to do is ignore your feelings. Anger, nerves and hurt are undeniable emotions. But instead of getting wrapped up in how you feel, think of your feelings as tip-offs that there is something you need to pay attention to. Feelings are like your internal hazard lights, they flash up to tell you to aim your energies and attention in a more positive direction.

Each time you chose positive thoughts over negative ones you are a step closer to higher confidence. Habits aren't always easy to break, but it's your choice. You can continue to live life in a negative frame of mind or you can chose to live life in a positive frame of mind.

Summary

Every time a thought enters your head or you experience something in your life, you should see it as a new opportunity for you to take control. So the next time you have a chance to decide how to react, think to yourself: 'How am I going to respond to this new opportunity?' Is it really worth giving up your mental health and happiness by continuing to choose a negative outcome? If you choose to take the path of negativity, then you will be focusing all your energies and attention on the problem and this will prevent you from raising your levels of confidence.

When you choose positive thinking, you lessen your chances of experiencing depression and low self-esteem. Positive thinking will also permeate other areas of your life – it is wonderfully infectious. And if you raise your own self-esteem and become more confident, the people around you will benefit as well. Not only will you be an inspirational person to be with, you'll also inspire your family and friends with your positive words and encouragement. Isn't that a fantastic idea?

Many people think negatively because this is what they are used to doing and they have been surrounded by negativity all of their lives. Even if this is the case for you, you still have a choice. It only takes a few seconds to change your reaction and how you feel. Each time you choose a positive response, you will feel the effect. You will instantly feel better about yourself and remain feeling positive.

Our internal dialogue is second nature to us, so much so that we don't even realize it's there most of the time. As soon as you notice how much you think, you'll start to notice how many of your thoughts are negative. Some of my clients have actually told me that once they started monitoring their thoughts, they realized that over 80 per cent of them were negative.

As I explained earlier, each time a negative, sceptical or pessimistic thought enters your head, you have a choice. You can choose to follow your usual negative train of thought, or you can choose to follow a more positive one – it really is up to you.

> *'The unfortunate thing about this world is that good habits are so much easier to give up than bad ones.'*
> — Somerset Maugham, English dramatist and novelist

8

Use the Power of Your Mind

'Imagination is more important than knowledge.' — Albert Einstein, scientist

magination is the key to learning and experiencing many things in life. For example, the scientist Albert Einstein used his imagination to project himself out among the planets where he could ride around on moonbeams and learn about the universe. His ability to use his imagination allowed him to become a giant among intellectuals.

How much do you use your imagination?

We all imagine ourselves in certain places or situations. But some of us use our imagination more than others. Remember when you started a new relationship or were due to go out on a date with someone new? Before you even left the house, you would have played the evening through in your mind wondering what would happen or where things would go. Maybe you still daydream in the same way about a relationship you may have one day. If you are due to present an important piece of work to your boss, you will probably use your imagination to predict how it will be received.

It is claimed that we do 70 per cent of our learning in the first six years of our life, as our ability to absorb information and new experiences is far greater then. This is also the time when our imagination is at its most fertile; we need a good imagination in order to learn quickly and easily. Therefore we need to place greater importance on having a lively imagination and take time to stimulate it and develop it into adulthood.

Many parents encourage their children's imagination as they know that having an active mind is the same as having an open mind – and open-minded children learn about and experience life more fully. I believe that if you use and stretch your mind throughout your life, it will help you develop a strong memory, and allow you to recall information faster and more accurately.

> 'Imagination rules the world.'
> — Benjamin Disraeli, British statesman

People's memories appear to deteriorate as they get older, but this is mainly due to the fact that we stop using our imagination rather than the fact that we are ageing. When we use our imagination we think in pictures. Thinking visually helps us remember things more easily. As elderly people gradually use their imagination less, they lose their range of pictures for recalling events, hence they seem to forget a lot of information quickly.

Meditation for relaxation

A good imagination is essential if you want to relax your mind and body. There are many techniques you can use do this, but the most effective and popular is meditation. This allows you to imagine yourself in a beautiful place, for example the beach, the countryside, at your favourite place or somewhere you associate with feeling good. While you are concentrating on thinking about this special place, your body and mind relaxes and you feel the warmth and the glow of positive energy from the experience.

EXERCISES

Below are useful exercises for relaxation and developing your imagination. They can be used when you are feeling anxious, nervous or your confidence is low. They are especially useful if you need to calm yourself down and focus your mind before entering a challenging situation.

BREATHING MEDITATION

1. Sit comfortably and close your eyes. Allow your mind to wander. Note how many thoughts run through your head. You'll probably notice there is a large number. Ignore them and concentrate instead on your breathing.

2. Breathe in through your nose, and as you are doing so think to yourself 'breathe in'. Then exhale and breathe out through your mouth, and as you are doing so think 'breathe out'.

3. Your mind will probably wander but don't stop breathing and saying 'breathe in' and 'breathe out' to yourself. Give this your attention and simply notice what you're thinking about.

4. After a few minutes or when you are ready, you can start to think

about opening your eyes. Do this gently, move your body slowly so that you can start to think about coming back to reality. You should feel refreshed and relaxed.

VISUALIZATION

1. Lie down in a comfortable, warm place. Make sure it is quiet and that you will not be disturbed. Close your eyes and concentrate on your breathing. Take deep breaths in and out, regulating your breathing so that you are relaxed. Breathe in through your nose and out through your mouth. When you are totally relaxed, start to think of a place that makes you feel happy and relaxed. Below are some examples:

- A beautiful beach.
- The countryside.
- Where you went on your honeymoon.
- A favourite place you visited as a child.
- Your garden.
- In your mum's arms.
- In the bath.

2. Focus on your special place and explore it in your mind: what it looks like, what colours you see, the smells and sounds that surround you. Note what is happening to your body when you are thinking about this place. Do you feel butterflies in your stomach? Does your pulse-rate quicken? Does your breathing pattern change? Do you find you are smiling without realizing it?

You can do both these exercises anywhere: in bed, in the bath, in fact any place where you can get a quiet five minutes. This is your very special area in your mind, somewhere that is totally private. No one can enter your head and ruin this imaginary moment for you, so use this technique as often as you want.

Mental rehearsal and results

None of us takes enough time out in the day to allow ourselves time to think things through or switch off. In this fast-paced world we live in, if you are seen to be switching off for a few minutes, it is assumed you are slacking or not concentrating on your work. When I was a child, my school report said I was 'easily distracted'. This was always seen as a weakness, yet all I was doing was using my imagination by creating pictures in my mind to help me recall what I was learning. We should not prevent our imagination from running away with itself, it is healthy to allow it to roam free. It's like a form of mental exercise, after all, we exercise our bodies, so why not exercise our minds?

Young girls use their imagination when they dream of their wedding day, the dress they'll wear and what their future husband will be like. When kids play games in the playground, you can hear them talking to themselves, holding imaginary objects, driving imaginary cars, pushing imaginary prams and talking to imaginary friends. This is imagination at its most fertile.

Leonardo da Vinci vowed at the age of 12, that he would become one of the world's greatest artists and live amongst kings and princes. As a young boy, we know that Napoleon spent many a long day dreaming of how he would lead his troops to conquer Europe. As a child, the astronaut Neil Armstrong dreamed of how one day he would become well known in aviation history, and as a young boy, Henry Ford dreamed of how he could make an affordable car so that everyone could own one. The rest, as the saying goes, is history.

As all these examples show, imagination provides focus and helps us create our dreams. By exercising our imagination we keep it active, and an active imagination will help you build your confidence as it allows you to project yourself into the future and see a positive outcome for an event. The ability to rehearse allows us to create a positive outcome for ourselves and this helps us achieve our goals and do our best – all big confidence boosters.

Athletes mentally rehearse how their race, game or performance is going to go. Let's use sprinters as an example. They imagine themselves warming up for the race and then getting the call to position themselves in their starting blocks. They then mentally rehearse hearing the starter gun and pushing themselves out of their starting blocks and starting their sprint. They are using their imagination all the time to think the race through in infinite detail until they imagine themselves running over the line and winning the race. Athletes never mentally visualize themselves losing the race, they always rehearse winning in their minds. Olympic athletes and other professional sportspeople commonly use their imagination in this way – you often see them with their eyes closed just before a race.

So what happens in our brain when we use this technique? Whenever you carry out an action, such as hitting a tennis ball with a tennis racket, your body is reacting to what your brain is telling it to do. If your brain tells your body that you are going to hit the ball well, then the chances are that you will. If your brain tells your body that you are not very good at tennis, then you are sending negative messages to your body and you are more likely to hit a bad shot. The more you practise, the better your automatic programme will become.

It is true that if you practise your performance will improve. But it has been proved that if you also rehearse what you are going to do in your imagination it will vastly improve your physical performance. The fastest way to improve a skill is to combine mental and physical practice to the same degree. Recent scientific studies have shown that when you use your imagination to rehearse the successful completion of a task, you alter your mental programming and bring about chemical changes in your brain. These chemical changes form pathways in your brain so that when you carry out the act physically, the knowledge as to how to do it well is already formed. This means that you can use your imagination to form new habits.

The key to using this technique successfully is, of course, to imagine yourself carrying out the task or behaviour perfectly. Unfortunately, many people spend their lives imagining the worst and what they are most worried about happening to them. This also leads to the formation of patterns in our brains, but these are destructive rather than constructive. So you can see that if we constantly think about negative outcomes then they are likely to happen to us. We then start to say: 'Why does it always happen to me?' Which makes us believe even more emphatically that we are destined to fail or have bad things happen to us.

I believe that we get what we expect in life and that we attract what we expect to get. The woman who says: 'I am always tired', will probably always feel that way as this is what her body and mind expect. The man who says 'I can never get a girlfriend' will probably never get a girlfriend, as this is the aura he projects. The office worker who says she 'always gets a headache' will probably get a lot of headaches, as this is what her mind is telling her body to do. The man who says he 'hates Mondays' will probably have a bad day on a Monday as he is already expecting to have one.

This can affect our physical well-being too because medical research has proved that patients heal at the rate they expect to heal. This is a contentious issue but there is proof to show that your mental focus and attitude towards an illness does impact on your healing pattern.

You get what you expect to get

We all have extensive memory banks, which are full of memories, experiences and dreams. But it is the things that we think about most and fear the most that we tend to attract to us. Why is that?

If I say to you: 'Don't think of a blue elephant,' you will automatically think of a blue elephant – you can't help it. This is because the brain can't process negatives.

For example, someone buys a really expensive pair of glasses and, because he is worried about breaking them, keeps telling everyone: 'I don't want to break these glasses, they were really expensive.' Before long, he has sat on them or broken them. You've probably had a similar experience. You buy a new shirt or top and wear it out. But because you particularly like it, or because it's a pale colour, you start to worry that you are going to spill something on it. Before long you have a stain on your new top. You say to yourself: 'I knew it! I told you, it always happens to me.'

By saying to ourselves: 'I don't want this to happen,' we end up veering towards it because we cannot tell our minds not to do something. Our minds cannot move away from something only towards it, hence: 'Don't think of a blue elephant' leads you to do just that.

We also experience fear and other intense emotions via the power of our imagination. We imagine how it would be if we fell out with or lost a member of our family or one of our friends. We also imagine losing our car key, wallet and handbag. And we fear losing our partner's love and affection. The problem is that if we concentrate on losing something enough, the world can sometimes make it happen for us. If you become preoccupied with losing your partner, you could become jealous, reserved or defensive with them and end up damaging your relationship as a result. So rather than imagining the worst, concentrate on what you have. Use your mental energy to focus on how you want things to be and where you want your life to go. Focus your mind in a positive direction, not a negative one.

From now on, decide to create a new habit for yourself. Practise using your imagination to enhance your performance and build your confidence. Build your desire for greater confidence and self-esteem. Run this through your mind over and over again, mentally rehearsing how confident you really are. Some of the most confident people use this technique all the time, so why don't you do the same and see what it does for your confidence levels?

Take time to imagine yourself being successful at something you lack confidence in. Visualize how everything around you will look, sound and feel when you have this confidence. What will people say or do? What will you say? How will you say it? Really make the feeling of confidence strong. Imagine being successful the way that sports people do and this will plant positive thoughts in your unconscious mind and build your inner confidence for any situation you may encounter.

EXERCISE

This exercise will give you an in-built ability to overcome self-doubt and low confidence. To do it successfully, you need to use your imagination to create a good feeling about yourself. It needs to be so good, you can feel it in your body. When you experience that good feeling at its strongest, you need to capture it so you can recall it at the click of a finger.

The aim of the exercise is to get yourself to a peak of happiness, anchor it, then release the anchor as soon as the feeling begins to diminish. The next time you want to feel the happy feeling, use the anchor and remember the feeling. Anchoring is good to use at moments when you need a boost of positive energy, when you are nervous, when you're feeling low in confidence. By using your anchor, you will be able to feel relaxed and calm.

1. First, lie down in a comfortable, warm, quiet place. Make sure you will not be disturbed. Close your eyes and just concentrate on your breathing. Take deep breaths in and out and regulate your breathing so that you are totally relaxed. Take your time; this exercise requires all your attention to be effective.

2. Regulate your breathing to really relax your body; all your muscles and limbs need to feel loose and heavy as you entirely let go. Breathe in through your nose and out through your mouth. Do this for a couple of minutes. When you are totally relaxed, start to think of a place or a time that made you feel really happy. It could be somewhere you went as a child or a special place you have shared with your partner. Below are some examples:

   • A beautiful beach you visited on holiday.
   • A place in the country: a special forest or some breathtaking scenery.
   • The place you went on your honeymoon.

- A favourite place you visited as a child.
- Your garden.
- In a warm, scented bath.
- Christmas day or your birthday.

3. Wherever that special place or time is for you, recall it in great detail and really feel what you felt at the time. What does it look like? What can you see, smell or hear that makes the happy feeling really strong for you? Why does it make you feel happy when you think of this place? Who else, if anyone, is there? Notice what is happening in your body when you are thinking about this special place. Do you feel butterflies in your stomach? Does your pulse-rate quicken? Does your breathing pattern change? Do you find you are smiling without realizing it? Really think deeply about this place and recapture the happy feeling, right now. Don't rush this process, really experience the happiness it is making you feel right now.

4. What I would like you to do while you are thinking about this special moment or place in your life is to create your own 'anchor' or reminder of the feeling. This means that I want you to do something that will bring back the memory and the emotion. You can do this either with a gesture, or by pressing your earlobe or finger. It needs to be something you can do discreetly but which is unusual enough that it is unique to that special feeling. Here are some examples of what some people have used as anchors:

- Holding one wrist with the other hand.
- Holding or grabbing a finger on one hand with the other hand.
- Clasping the hands together.
- Squeezing one arm with the other hand.
- Crossing two fingers.
- Pressing both hands together.

It is best that you find an action that you feel happy with, something that feels comfortable and natural to you and something that you will remember as your anchor.

This may seem a strange thing to do at first, but do it as well as you can otherwise you'll never know if it works for you. It isn't that strange either: all you are doing is training your mind to remember the feelings associated with your anchor – it's simply a reminder. There are reminders all around you: music that reminds you of a particular time in your life, a smell that reminds you of someone you know and the sound of someone's laughter will bring back memories of a happy time.

If the anchor doesn't work the first time round, repeat the exercise until the good feeling becomes familiar and easy to recall at any time. The best thing is that you can do this exercise anywhere and at any time: in bed, in the bath, anywhere you can be quiet and undisturbed. Imagine how wonderful it will be to squeeze your arm or grasp your wrist and get that warm, safe, happy feeling again.

You get what you focus on

Have you noticed that when you decide to buy something, for example a particular make of car or a washing machine, that all of a sudden you see masses of adverts for that very item or you see cars like the one you want everywhere you go. Well it's certainly not just coincidence, it's also because you start to notice it more. It works along the same lines as 'what we expect, we get'. All of a sudden, you start looking for, and noticing, that very thing.

If you weren't looking for it before, you probably won't have noticed it, but now it is at the forefront of your mind you'll see it everywhere. A good example of this is when a relationship ends. To begin with, you are so wrapped up in your ex-partner that you don't notice anyone else. Consequently, you don't stand a chance of meeting someone new. The moment you drop the emotional attachment to your old love, your aura changes and you start to attract potential partners again. See if you can identify with any of the following occurrences.

- You think about someone you haven't seen for a long time and they ring you.

- You dream about someone and they contact you the next day.

- You start humming a really old song then you turn on the radio and it's playing.

- You think of a well-known person, and they're on the front page of your newspaper.

We think of these situations as remarkable coincidences, but like many other researchers and specialists in personal development, I believe there is a greater force at work than just coincidence. The author of *Creative Visualization*, Shakti Gawain, says that: 'Thought and feeling have their own magnetic energy, which attracts energy of a similar nature.' In a very general sense, it is said that whatever we give out to the universe we generally get back. If we want to achieve something, then we will achieve it. So the power of the mind combined with physical action is a very powerful formula for success.

Create a better memory

Research indicates that we never forget anything that has happened to us. Even information that we can't seem to recall is actually stored in our memory, the problem is only in accessing it. Although many people say they have a terrible memory and that they are forgetful, their memory is as good as the next person's. But if they keep telling themselves their memory is bad, they might start to convince themselves that it is true – then they may find their ability to recall information deteriorates even further.

If you start to say to yourself and others: 'I want to remember things' or 'I do remember things' then you are training your unconscious mind to help you remember. So, rather than saying: 'I'm terrible at remembering people's names', why not tell your unconscious mind: 'I am very good at remembering people's names' instead? You know this is the case, because when you forget something then remember it two days later it simply proves that you knew it all along. It is only anxiety and lack of confidence in your memory that makes it falter. If you start telling yourself that you have a good memory, you'll see that your ability to recall information dramatically improves.

Where there's a will, there's a way

If you think you don't have the will-power to change, think again. We often use our apparent lack of will-power to explain why our diet failed on day two or how we can't stop smoking. But your will is controlled by your thoughts and beliefs. If you believe you don't have the will-power, you will allow yourself to dwell on how great that cigarette or packet of biscuits will be rather than how fantastic you'll feel when you've lost weight or given up the habit.

If you think about it, will-power is simply the application of your mind to achieving a task. Will-power is all about mental energy and focus. You are in control of your mind, so it is you that is letting your mind run away with itself at times. So, having the will-power to build your own confidence, lose weight or give up smoking is entirely under your control. If you believe you can do it, you can. If you can build a picture of yourself doing it, then that will help. If you anchor the good feeling of giving up smoking and losing weight, you'll have a resource to call upon when you are tempted away from your goal.

Summary

In this chapter, I have highlighted the power of your mind in raising your confidence and getting what you want. It's your most valuable asset when building and maintaining a high level of confidence.

Take a moment to think about what you are thinking and feeling when you are low in confidence, nervous or in a state of fear. Do you allow your mind to convince itself that you are useless, that it'll all go wrong or that you're going to get hurt? Or do you imagine a positive outcome, begin to relax and start to believe you're going to be fine.

Look at these everyday examples of how we use the power of our mind to persuade ourselves to do things. Can you relate to any of these events?

1. You are sitting comfortably on your sofa watching your favourite film, when a nagging thought starts pressing you to go and sort out what you are going to wear to work the next day. You go and sort out your clothes, and you feel much better for being organized the following morning.

2. You know you need to clean out the car as it's a mess, but you're feeling tired. You somehow manage to persuade yourself to go and do it. The car is clean and clutter-free and you feel better knowing it is tidy.

3. You are at the water park and you are surrounded by huge water slides. You don't like the look of the steep 'kamikaze' slide, but you manage to persuade yourself to have a go on it. You come away feeling exhilarated and proud that you didn't lose your nerve.

4. You are supposed to be filling in your tax return as the deadline is looming. You keep putting it off, but you then decide that you might as well get it done. You finish filling it in, and feel a great sense of relief as you now know you will hit your deadline. You have a huge sense of achievement after completing this, because you have been dreading it.

All of these examples demonstrate that it is you who controls your mind, and that you have got the will-power you need to drive you to do whatever it is you want to do.

You can apply this theory to building your own confidence. When you have moments of doubt and feel that you are not in control, just remember that you are in control of your mind, and it can help you achieve whatever it is you want to achieve.

9

Your Body

'My philosophy has always been to help men and women feel comfortable and confident through the clothes they wear.'
— Giorgio Armani, fashion designer

The moment we meet people we start forming impressions about them. Some of our responses are conscious and some are unconscious. Experts believe that up to 80 per cent of a first impression is derived from body language: eye contact, posture, facial expressions and gestures. So we all give away as much about ourselves with our body language as we do with the words we speak.

You already know a lot more about body language than you think you do because you use it all the time to assess and interpret what people are really saying to you. But if you try to control it or become too aware of your own body language you can start to look false. Using positive body language can make you feel confident, as long as you are comfortable with it and it feels right to you. There are many subtle techniques you can adopt to make yourself feel and appear more confident. Once you get to know what they are, they will become second nature, and they will happen automatically.

The most expressive part of the body is the face. Someone who is nervous or lacking in confidence often appears tense and serious, leading others to think they are unfriendly or sullen. If you meet someone new and their expression is unwelcoming, it does not necessarily mean that they are not pleased to see you. It is more likely that they are preoccupied or on edge for some reason. Always consider this and let your instincts guide you rather than jumping to conclusions.

If you feel anxious, be especially aware of your facial expressions. Remember to smile, because this will instantly help you relax and appear more approachable. If you are feeling uncomfortable, a smile can make you seem false, so make sure you smile with your eyes as well as your mouth. You can practise this in front of a mirror. Simply relax your facial muscles then smile with your whole face until it feels right. This is invaluable if you are going to an event that you are nervous about or feel will be challenging for you.

Smiling

Your smile is one of the most powerful tools you have for gaining an instant rapport with someone. It gives others the message that you are a friendly, open and confident person. A friend of mine did this on the London Underground and she said that initially people glared at her as if she was a little crazy, but soon after she was really comfortable with this and found almost all the people she smiled at smiled back, which made her feel great. I read this poem recently and loved it so much that I thought I would share it with you.

Smiling is contagious

Smiling is contagious, you catch it like the flu,
When someone smiled at me today, I started smiling too.
I passed around the corner, and someone saw my grin,
When he smiled I realized, I'd passed it onto him.
I thought about that smile, then I realized its worth,
A single smile, just like mine could travel round the earth.
So if you feel a smile begin, don't leave it undetected
Let's start an epidemic quick and get the world infected!
— Anonymous

The next time you are out, notice how many people are smiling as they walk down the street or talk to people. You may not see many. Watch people when they smile to see if they are using their eyes as well. A genuine smile lights up someone's whole face. Not-so-genuine smiles only come from the corners of the mouth.

Eye Contact

Eye contact is also a major source of information about someone and its use or avoidance can signal an instant welcome or rebuttal. If someone does not make much eye contact, it can either mean they are shy or not very interested in what you are saying. When making eye contact with someone new, keep it balanced. Look at someone's eyes while they are talking to show that you are listening, but glance away when you are talking so that they have the chance to look at you. If the situation is intense, look at the bridge of someone's nose rather than straight at their eyes to reduce the intensity of your gaze.

The way you use your eyes can really influence people and situations, so this is something you need to practise and get used to in both social and work situations. If you are with a small group of people, make sure you glance at everyone and get some kind of eye-contact with each person so you can be accepted – and show you accept – everyone present. This shows you are someone who wants to include others and be included by people. It's particularly useful when you are meeting new people. It gives the message that you are confident too. People who lack confidence often bow their heads and look at the floor, which means others will avoid talking to them. To overcome shyness and cope when you are feeling low in confidence, lift your head and look around the room so that you can make eye contact with people.

If you are shy, do this the next time you go to a party or meeting. Learn by watching how others make eye contact and use body language and copy their techniques. Just acting as if you are confident will make you appear so and will make you feel it too.

Gestures

Hand and arm gestures can make you appear enthusiastic, expressive and upbeat. Use them in moderation and at a level you are comfortable with, because you can look nervous if they are overdone. Avoid rubbing your hands together, twiddling your fingers, fiddling with your jewellery or playing with your sleeves, as this gives the impression that you are nervous or tense. It may also be interpreted as proof that you are not telling the truth, which could be very damaging in a business or interview situation.

Using wide, open gestures gives the impression that you are an open person. However, small gestures bring the listener's attention to what you are saying. Whatever way you choose to use them, gestures will add to your presence and make you appear more confident.

Posture

Your posture and stance can also be a strong indication of your level of confidence. Your posture – whether you lean towards someone or away from them – shows how interested you are in someone and how much attention you are giving to what they are saying. It can also reflect your status within a group and how well accepted you are by those around you.

When we are feeling low, we tend to want to shy away from others and hide. We stand or sit with our heads bowed and bodies stooped as if we are literally shrinking and getting smaller so people won't notice us.

But when we are feeling confident, lively and up-beat, we push out our chests and hold our heads up. We broaden our stance and take up more space to make ourselves appear as powerful as possible.

However, if you just adopt a confident posture without feeling confident inside, you may just appear stiff and awkward. If you want to adopt a positive posture at a time when you are feeling low or lacking in confidence, simply relax your whole body. By doing this, you will find that you adopt a naturally confident posture and appear much more convincing to others.

Motivation

Different things motivate different people, and only you will know what really inspires you. When you feel motivated about something, you are full of life, energy and confidence. There are times when your energy level is high and times when it is low, so it helps for you to get to know your own rhythms and learn how to generate motivation for yourself or overcome low points. This is particularly important for work situations when you are required to perform regardless of how you are feeling.

To access feelings of motivation, find somewhere you can sit quietly and undisturbed for a few minutes, then think of a time when you were really motivated. Allow the feeling of motivation to grow and use your imagination to recreate the situation, what you saw, heard and felt at that time. Wait until you are feeling really motivated, then anchor it. Create a positive phrase you can say to yourself that will raise your energy levels further and make you feel positive and empowered. Use your posture to make yourself look and act as if you are feeling good and very motivated, and the feelings will follow.

Health

Today, we all rush around from place to place leaving ourselves no time to relax. Pressure, stress and the sense that we need to be the best seems to run our lives. In many workplaces today, staff feel insecure about job security and frequently worry about the possibility of redundancy. Because of this threat, many employees believe they have to work twice as hard as their colleagues and don't take lunch or other breaks during the day when they can focus and take time out.

Eventually, this lack of self-care affects our mental and physical health. Exercise, relaxation and eating a balanced diet go some way to combating a demanding lifestyle. If you miss meals, you may well spend more time working, but you may be less productive as a result. Lack of food, fresh air, daylight and rest will leave you tired, hungry and irritable and reduce your confidence and concentration levels.

These days, we rely on packaged foods for speed and convenience. But this can just result in a vicious circle in which you crave high-sugar foods, resulting in fatigue and the desire for more foods like this. What most people don't realize is that a poor diet and lack of exercise act as mood suppressants, so we get low, sometimes depressed, which means our confidence and self-esteem dip and increase our bad feelings about ourselves.

Looking after ourselves is proof that we value and care for ourselves. This raises our esteem and confidence. Eating well, exercising and generally giving ourselves time to relax is crucial to self-confidence; by looking after ourselves we gain a sense of well-being, have more energy, feel more motivated and value ourselves more.

There are many guides to good diet and we all know that we should eat a balanced diet that provides us with a range of vitamins and minerals. Drinking plenty of water and cutting down on caffeine will reduce your chances of getting a headache, while avoiding high-fat and high-sugar foods will help to regulate your mood.

Making time to exercise

The same is true for exercise. It isn't everyone's favourite subject, but before you're tempted to gloss over this section, let me tell you how exercise and your confidence are linked. Exercise releases endorphins in the brain and these, in turn, raise your mood, self-esteem and confidence. Being fit helps us to become happier so you need to find a form of exercise that you enjoy and can fit into your routine. It doesn't have to be expensive or time-consuming. It could be anything, from taking a walk each day, going on a bike ride or for a swim. Whatever you choose, taking time away from work, especially if it mostly involves being in an office and sitting at a desk, gives you a much-needed break. If you're not an exercise fan, fit short bursts of exercise into your day by walking up the stairs, gardening, parking your car further away from the office or train station and going for a walk at lunchtime.

EXERCISE

Make a decision to eat healthily and exercise regularly for seven days so you can discover for yourself how this impacts your overall health. Notice whether you sleep better, have fewer mood swings and whether your confidence levels rise. Keep a diary of what happens.

- Eat five portions of fruit and vegetables every day.
- Drink eight glasses of water a day.
- Moderate your alcohol intake.
- Exercise for at least 30 minutes a day.
- Get eight hours' sleep every night.
- Make time to relax and meditate for an hour every day.
- Ask family and friends for support.
- Make sure you have plenty of laughter each day.

Emotions

Medical research indicates that emotional stress produces high levels of toxins in our blood. This proves that what we think and feel has an impact on our body chemistry. It is believed that the toxins we create as a result of experiencing fear, anxiety, anger and stress can make us ill, although the extent depends on the level of emotion experienced. Medical conditions such as IBS (Irritable Bowel Syndrome), migraine, asthma, eczema and many other conditions can be triggered by stress.

In fact, these days your doctor is as likely to talk to you about your lifestyle as your symptoms when you are ill. This is because your state of mind is directly linked to your health. Illness can also be a result of unresolved inner turmoil due to people internalizing their worries and fears rather than releasing them.

But it is not just our conscious mind that can affect our health, our unconscious mind can be just as influential. Have you ever been unwell on a day when you had to do something you found challenging? To combat this tendency, you need to accept your challenges and boost your confidence so you believe you can meet them. This will remove the need to avoid certain events. The other thing you need to do is to convince your body that it is in great shape, and that illness is not the proper response to fear or lack of self-esteem. Instead, you need to think healthy thoughts and focus your attention on being well.

Stress

Stress is part of life and we all feel stressed at some time. When you are under a lot of stress your heart rate increases, your breathing becomes shallow and your muscles tense up. Stress can make you think irrationally, feel pressurized and really low in confidence. It can be caused by many things, from going on holiday or starting a new job, to losing a loved one.

Stress in small bursts isn't necessarily a bad thing: it provides us with energy to help us perform well when we are nervous and adrenalin for speed and strength when we need to escape danger. However, being frequently over-stressed is bad for us and it leads to health problems – both mental and physical – in the long run.

The first step you need to take to deal with stress is to recognize it in the first place. It can present itself in many ways, not all of them obvious. Symptoms range from the physical, such as tension in the shoulders, headaches or a general feeling of lethargy, to the mental, such as forgetfulness, confusion and feeling overloaded with information. It is important not to blame yourself for experiencing stress, because it's a signal from within that you need to take greater care of yourself. Relax and wind down in a way you find effective or use techniques such as relaxation to deal with the situation.

Stress and confidence

Confidence building is difficult when you are under stress because when there are problems and challenges, it becomes very tempting to hide from situations that you find stressful rather than dealing with them head on. The problem though, is that stressors won't go away if you don't face them. Once you do that you can use your own personal methods to deal with it should it recur.

Sometimes, we dwell too much on an event rather than just throwing ourselves in at the deep end and getting on with it. If we did, we'd certainly build our confidence much faster. Positive action is a liberating tool and worth keeping as an option you can use at any time. In order to help deal with stress we also need to control our thought processes (see Chapter 6: Your Thoughts and How You Feel) as this will help you stay in a positive state of mind when you deal with a challenging situation. Our perceptions of a situation alter depending on how we actually feel, so if our confidence is low, we lack self-esteem or we feel stressed or down, we are far more likely to see a situation negatively. This results in more stress as we begin to feel we can't cope, that life is unfair and that nothing is ever easy. Warding off stress reduces the chances of feeling this way and makes the challenges we face in daily life far easier to approach positively.

It is a good idea to know the kind of situation that causes you to feel stressed so you can learn to recognize it before it happens and deal with it in your own way. You may even learn to look at the situation differently next time. That way, nerves about giving a presentation become a sign of excitement, and fear a sign that you are broadening your skills and experience.

Mastering, and indeed surviving, what life throws at us is a constant challenge, but if we convert stress into positive energy then it's a great help. Remember, everyone needs some stress, it's only when it becomes overwhelming, relentless and damaging that you need to redress the balance, look after yourself better and make moves to reduce its impact on your life.

Self-esteem and body image

Confidence is all about how much you like yourself. If you have high self-esteem, you are more likely to have a healthy, confident attitude to life. In Western society, much of our self-esteem comes from our body image. However, as the media is full of images of people with the perfect life and perfect body we constantly receive subliminal messages that we too could be perfect, if only we bought a particular beauty product or went on a specific diet. This type of communication brings an amazing amount of pressure to most people's lives: pressure to lose weight, wear certain clothes, spend money and behave in a certain way.

This pressure affects both men and women – and more worryingly young boys and girls. Research shows that women want to be slimmer and men want to be more muscular than ever before, leading to cosmetic surgery, unhealthy diets and excessive spending.

We tend to forget that these perfect images are impossible for most of us to achieve because the media covers up any imperfection with clever photography and computer-manipulation of the photographs. The problem is that most of us are in constant pursuit of an ideal, which leaves us feeling depressed when we don't achieve the end result. This leads to poor self-esteem and reduces our confidence.

Many of us think we are not attractive because we are not perfect. Many of us have not learned to accept ourselves as we are, and this makes us unhappy and damages our confidence. We need to remind ourselves that there are many ways to be attractive and that there is no need to conform to the ideal presented by the media. How many of us at some point in our lives have got chatting to someone really good looking only to find that we have nothing in common with them. Because we are bored or don't like someone, we stop finding them attractive. Which goes to prove what we already know really – personality outweighs physical beauty when it comes to a relationship with someone.

We all have days when we don't feel as happy with ourselves as we would like. In fact self-image has a major influence on our confidence. How often do you wake up, look in the mirror and think: 'Oh no, look at the state of me. I look old, tired, wrinkly, fat ...' All these negative thoughts stay with you throughout the day, which brings down your confidence. Instead, start to appreciate and admire yourself. Concentrate on what you do like about yourself so a new self-image filters down into your unconscious. As you start to appreciate yourself more, your confidence will increase as well and this will be reflected in the way you look, feel, dress and act.

Summary

It is much better to accept yourself for who you are and what you look like, than to waste energy and happiness on constantly trying to be something you're not or like someone else. Get the feel-good factor by exercising, eating a healthy diet and doing what makes you happy, and remember, you need a healthy mind as well as a healthy body in order to be happy. The attitude you have about yourself and life determines who you are today. Focus and act upon your strengths rather than dwelling on your weaknesses. If you lack confidence in your appearance then you will convey lack of confidence in yourself and people may not feel comfortable around you. Start believing in yourself and who you are, and as soon as you do this you will feel much more confident.

10

Life Isn't A Dress Rehearsal

'The really great make you feel that you too can become great.' — Mark Twain, 19th-century author

Given the right information, support tools and guidance, anyone can fulfill their potential and be confident. Many people have a lot to give and so much talent, but they just don't have the confidence to make the most of themselves. I believe you can succeed in whatever it is you want to do. Being successful takes confidence and a positive attitude. Believe in yourself, because if you believe you can do something, you will do it.

Don't discount your successes or failures. You need to take responsibility for what happens to you in life. Obviously there are some things that are not within your control, but you need to recognize what has happened to you as a result of something you have done. Rather than blame other people, the world (or the weather!) for your situation, look at yourself to see how you might have – unintentionally – brought about the event yourself. You need to be proactive about making changes: if you are not happy with your current environment, whether it be your professional or personal life, decide to make changes or leave it altogether. But make sure you are not just running away from your problems or yourself in the process.

Be careful who your friends are

Make friends with people who are positive and successful. Remember, if you spend a lot of time with negative people, you'll become negative yourself. If you spend time with confident, positive people you'll become confident and positive, too. Try to build in some time to spend with people you admire; people who can give you advice and who may be in a position to be your mentor. This could be someone who has confidence and is successful in many or all (if they are lucky) areas of their life. Confidence breeds success, just as success breeds confidence. Look at what they have done, what they believe and how they have approached set-backs and decisions and see what you can learn from these. What aspect of their behaviour, strategy or attitude could you use in your own quest for success? Make sure it is in keeping with your own values and personality though.

Leave your baggage in the past

Forget the negatives from your past and work on removing any emotional baggage you are carrying around with you. Learn from your mistakes, then move on. Your past has happened for a reason. Most things that have happened to you have happened because of decisions you made – or maybe did not make. Acknowledge this, but don't dwell on the 'mistake' aspect. Instead, concentrate on your future and what you can do to be successful in the present. Stay focused on your confidence: the more attention you give it, the more it will improve. Take more risks and do all the things you have been scared or reluctant to do in the past. Allow yourself to learn, grow and develop. Learn something new – every day if possible – that will enrich your knowledge and improve your skills.

Change takes time

If you want something, you have to work at it and it's the same with confidence-building. If you want confidence enough, you'll work to achieve it. Strive for a balance in everything you do in both your professional and personal life. Action and persistence are key when building your confidence. Successful people know that they have to keep trying in order to achieve their goals.

> 'The way to succeed is to double your failure rate.'
> — Thomas J Watson, founder of IBM

Change takes effort and persistence. That's probably why it's so easy to give up when you first set out to learn or achieve something new. How many times have you promised yourself you'll go to the gym then don't do it? The choice is yours: are you a quitter or an achiever? Thomas Edison had to invent thousands of light bulbs that didn't work until he found the one that did. The actor, Christopher Reeve, who was paralysed in an accident, pushes the boundaries of his life daily as he tries to regain movement in his limbs. The singer Julio Iglesias was involved in a car accident when he was twenty years old which left him paralysed from the waist down. Through persistence and determination he managed to regain the use of his legs. He did it because he believed he was meant to walk again.

You are who you think you are

Where you are today has generally been dictated by your thoughts, decisions and actions and so it stands to reason that where you are in five years time will depend on you – what you believe about yourself, where you decide you want to be and what you want to be doing. We all know that life seems to pass at a phenomenal rate, so make sure you appreciate every moment for what it is.

Being confident is about liking and valuing yourself. This is what you'll experience when you have high self-confidence:

- A belief in your own ability.
- The courage to achieve what you want.
- The belief that you are as capable as everyone else.
- The ability to be secure and relaxed about yourself.
- The ability to act confidently even when you are feeling low.
- The ability to acknowledge your mistakes, learn from them and move on.
- A lack of concern about what other people think of you.
- Freedom from intimidation.
- The ability to talk to anyone about anything.
- The ability to focus on appreciating and enjoying the present.
- The ability to put your attention on your goals and make them happen.

To achieve this, you'll need to maintain a positive attitude. Your life is in your hands and the quality of your life depends on you and the value you place on it. Life can feel worthless unless you give it value. It is up to you whether you decide to give life the value it so deserves. You are in control of whether you take life by the scruff of the neck and live it or merely exist.

Just as you can choose how to react to events in your life, so you can choose how confident you want to be. Whatever effort you expend today will create results tomorrow, so the sooner you start, the better and faster your confidence will grow.

Congratulate yourself on what you have achieved so far. You have recognized that you have the power to make changes in your life: changes that will allow you to build your confidence. When your confidence is low, remember that you are not alone and that the feeling is not permanent. As you learn to increase your confidence you will feel benefits and see results in every area of your life. And, even better, you'll have an impact on the lives of those around you at the same time. How wonderful and fulfilling to know that not only are you improving your own well-being and happiness, but you are also making those around you feel the same way.

Live in the present

Happy, confident people strive to live life in the present and focus their attention on what is happening now. As adults we have learned to let past regrets and future concerns cloud our present. We can all look back and regret decisions and actions we took, but we cannot change our past, and if we continue to beat ourselves up over things that we should or should not have done, then we will never feel totally good about ourselves. Our self-esteem will remain low and our confidence will dwindle.

When you next start to feel insecure and low in confidence, ask yourself these two questions:

1. What am I worried about?

2. Does it really matter?

If you find that you are worrying about something that does really matter, then do something about it, talk to someone who can help you deal with it and solve your problem. If it isn't important, let it go.

The power of positive thinking

Remember that the words you use affect how you feel. Next time you find yourself facing a difficult situation, rather than thinking of it as a really big problem, try to look at it as a challenge that you can overcome. When we believe we have a problem to deal with, we automatically approach it with negative energy and start to feel stressed. But if you see your problem as a challenge, you approach it with positive energy, which helps you solve it faster. Did you know that the Chinese word for crisis is the same as the word for opportunity? What a great way to look at challenges.

You know now that your thoughts are very powerful. By changing your thoughts from negative to positive ones, you can alter the quality of your life and create a positive environment around yourself. Negativity only attracts more negativity, so stay positive and this will give you a positive outcome and a better experience of the event itself.

When you are in the process of making changes to the way you think and behave it can be very easy to find excuses to put things off. Generally, people who lack confidence will often find that they surround themselves with people who zap their energy for one reason or another. People like this are not going to be able to help and support you in your quest for greater confidence. You need to identify people around you who can help you and encourage you to achieve your goal to build your confidence. Once your confidence starts to increase you need to look at how you can maintain that level of confidence for good! Ask yourself:

- Who is it that I would choose to talk to when I am feeling unconfident?
- Which of the people around me make me feel good about myself?
- Who can help me when I can't sort out a problem?
- Which people close to me do I gain inspiration from?

In deciding to build your confidence you are choosing to form a new habit, the habit of being confident. We all have habits we find hard to break, but unless we can actually see the benefit to us of change, we will find it hard to motivate ourselves into action.

Make time for yourself

If you have a busy lifestyle you are probably not getting enough quality time to yourself, so now is the time to change this too. Sooner or later your manic lifestyle will bring you down. This is why you need to regain control and start to manage your time more effectively. If you are wondering when you are going to get enough time to concentrate on building your confidence and take time for yourself, then take a look at the list of ideas below which may help you to manage your time more effectively.

- Write a task list for yourself. Use a notebook, a noticeboard or pin board somewhere visible and accessible so you can keep a running list of things that you need to do. If you use a diary or Filofax then dedicate an area within it for your 'to do' list.

- When writing your list, ask yourself if you really need to do this task, and whether someone else can help you with it or do it for you. Be ruthless, maybe scrubbing the stair carpet could wait for a week, and painting the spare room or digging the garden could hold off for a while.

- Prioritize your tasks in order of importance and urgency and put the most pressing ones at the top. These will probably be the tasks that are causing you the most stress, so get them done first so that you experience a sense of relief sooner rather than later.

- Say no to things that you don't want to do or you don't need to do. If you are saying yes to something when you want to say no, then you are not saying what you really mean. This will no doubt affect your self-respect and confidence. We have all struggled with 'no' at some point in our lives, but some of us battle with this little word on a daily basis. If you are carrying out something begrudgingly and with resentment because you haven't managed to be honest, then you will only be making yourself unhappy and will not carry out the task to your best ability. If saying no is difficult for you, practise saying the word to yourself when you are alone. Visualize the situation in which you may have to say no, and imagine yourself saying it. Remember the power that the mind exercises and how you are in control! The first time you say no may feel scary, but you'll soon get used to it. Don't abuse it though, just use it when you really mean it, then you will feel proud of yourself, which will help you feel confident and enable you to manage your time more effectively. This way you will have time for yourself to practise becoming the amazing confident person you are going to become.

Do not feel guilty about creating more time for yourself. Guilt can be destructive and is a very unproductive emotion. We all feel guilt, but women often feel more guilt than men. A familiar female guilt trip surrounds the conflict between their children and their career. Guilt can deplete your confidence and self-esteem because you are eroding your feelings of self-worth, so ditch that guilt right away.

Keep learning

Remember to indulge in a spot of people-watching. You can learn a lot about people by observing how they go about doing things, saying things and behaving towards others. Focus on people you admire, maybe a confident person in your office.

Use children as role-models for letting go of the past. Even if they have the odd run-in, they soon get over it and find ways to play together again. They don't hold grudges, dwell upon their mistakes or beat themselves up over things they've done or said. They tend to see the beauty in life and see life in its purest form. Children don't care if you are black or white, old or young, rich or poor, they don't judge people, they take them at face value. The difference between children and adults is that when children become upset or unhappy, they get upset and then move on quite quickly to feeling good again. They don't dwell on the behaviour or label themselves as failures, they get on with their lives.

Summary

So you see, you were confident once, because you were a child, and this is a quality that you can quite easily regain once you recognize that it is only you who is preventing yourself from being confident. A recent survey was taken of pensioners. In the survey they were asked if they had any regrets about their life, and, if so, what they were. The number one regret was: 'I wish I had done more with my life.' Make sure you don't fall into this category, by starting to build your own confidence today so you can make the most of this very valuable precious life you have. You see, you really are your own confidence coach; you just didn't realize it.

> 'You have to be a dedicated person. You have to want to do it more than any other person. You have to want to be number one. Then you have to have the ability.'
> — Mario Andretti, Formula 1 racing driver

Quotes of Confidence

Just as much as we see in others we have in ourselves.
– William Hazlitt, English essayist and critic

It's not who you are that holds you back, it's who you think you're not.
– Anonymous

We have to learn to be our own best friends because we fall too easily into the trap of being our own worst enemies.
– Roderick Thorp, *Rainbow Drive*

Success comes in cans, not can'ts.
– Anonymous

Put your future in good hands – your own.
– Anonymous

If you really put a small value upon yourself, rest assured that the world will not raise your price.
– Anonymous

It is not the mountain we conquer but ourselves.
– Edmund Hillary, mountaineer

Confidence comes not from always being right but from not fearing to be wrong.
– Peter T. Mcintyre

You have to expect things of yourself before you can do them.
– Michael Jordan, American basketball player

Aerodynamically the bumblebee shouldn't be able to fly, but the bumblebee doesn't know that so it goes on flying anyway.
– Mary Kay Ash, writer and entrepreneur

Confidence is a habit that can be developed by acting as if you already had the confidence you desire to have.
– Brian Tracy, American personal development coach

When there is no enemy within, the enemies outside cannot hurt you.
– African Proverb

We probably wouldn't worry about what people think of us if we could know how seldom they do.
– Olin Miller, writer

Oliver Wendell Holmes once attended a meeting in which he was the shortest man present. 'Dr. Holmes,' quipped a friend, 'I should think you'd feel rather small among us big fellows.' 'I do,' retorted Holmes, 'I feel like a dime among a lot of pennies.'
– Anonymous

'You have brains in your head.
You have feet in your shoes.
You can steer yourself in any direction you choose.
You're on your own.
And you know what you know.
You are the guy who'll decide where to go.'
– Dr Seuss

Further Reading

Being Happy! Andrew Matthews, Media Masters Pte Ltd (1989)

Chicken Soup for the Soul. Jack Canfield and Mark Victor Hansen, Vermilion (2000)

The Confidence to be Yourself. Dr Brian Roet, Piatkus Books (2001)

The 7 Habits of Highly Effective People. Stephen R. Covey, Simon & Schuster (1999)

Self Esteem. Gael Lindenfield, HarperCollins (2000)

Stop Thinking & Start Living. Richard Carlson, HarperCollins (1997)

Index

Acknowledgements

To my beautiful children Georgia and Mienna, may you find all the confidence you need to fulfil your dreams. The same goes to you Alex and Charlie, my gorgeous niece and nephew.

To you, Mum and Dad, my confidence is down to you. I cannot put into words how much I love you both. If I could bottle the tremendous amount of love, guidance and support you have given and continue to give me, and share it with everyone else, then what a wonderful world we would all live in. Thank you.

To my sister Kate O'Hara, thank you for the massive amount of love and encouragement you have given me throughout my life, you always make me feel like I can do anything and I certainly know that you can. Thanks for all you have done for me big sis and you, too, Neal 'Elvis' O'Hara.

To Phil, you are an amazing person, a big thank you for all you have done for your family and me over the years.

To Ian, thank you for all the love and support you have given me. Thanks for nagging me to get to the computer and write this book rather than sit and have a glass of wine or three on the terrace.

To Lottie and Corrina, you both bring me so much happiness, laughter and reassurance. You are my mentors, my friends and my agony aunts! Here's to many more happy times together.

To Lou, Helen, Ian, Gwen, Rudi, Christine, DB, Mags, Dobie, Plum, Steve and to all my other friends and colleagues – you know who you are – thank you for being you.